THE SPLENDID VISION

THE SPLENDID VISION

READING A BUDDHIST SUTRA

RICHARD S. COHEN

COLUMBIA UNIVERSITY PRESS

NEW YORK

COLUMBIA UNIVERSITY PRESS

Publishers Since 1893

New York   Chichester, West Sussex

cup.columbia.edu

Copyright © 2012 Columbia University Press

All rights reserved

Library of Congress Cataloging-in-Publication Data

Sarvatathagatadhisthanasatvavalokanabuddhaksetrasandarsanavyuha. English.

The splendid Vision : reading a Buddhist sutra / Richard S. Cohen.

p.   cm.

Includes English translation from Tibetan and Sanskrit sources.

Includes bibliographical references and index.

ISBN 978-0-231-15668-4 (cloth : alk. paper) —

ISBN 978-0-231-15669-1 (pbk.) —

ISBN 978-0-231-52752-1 (electronic)

I. Cohen, Richard S., 1963-   II. Title.

BQ2240.S3922E5   2012

294.3'85—DC23

2011027733

Columbia University Press books are printed on permanent and durable acid-free paper.

This book was printed on paper with recycled content.

Printed in the United States of America

c 10 9 8 7 6 5 4 3 2 1

p 10 9 8 7 6 5 4 3 2 1

References to Internet Web sites (URLs) were accurate at the time of writing.
Neither the author nor Columbia University Press is responsible for URLs that
may have expired or changed since the manuscript was prepared.

DESIGN & TYPESETTING *by* VIN DANG

FOR MY PARENTS,
BERNICE AND DAVID COHEN

CONTENTS

PREFACE

Once upon a time, maybe fifteen hundred years ago, high in the Himalaya Mountains, a man and a woman hired a scribe to copy a Mahayana sutra. The man was named Shulkshina, the woman, Shulivujna. And the sutra they had copied was entitled *The Splendid Vision in Which One Observes Living Beings and Reveals Buddhafields Through the Empowerment of All Tathagatas*.

Scholars of Indian history often lament the lack of detailed information available to them. Sources arrive from ancient days incomplete, devoid of context, and damaged. In this regard, the *Splendid Vision* sutra is no different. Many details we would like to know about this text's origins and patrons are lost. We cannot say whether Shulkshina and Shulivujna were Iranian or Chinese, Indian or Afghani. We do not know their ages, their wealth, or their social standing. Were they husband and wife? Brother and sister? Or did their relationship lie, simply, in their shared devotion to the buddha?

Still, although we cannot recover the intimate details of Shulkshina's and Shulivujna's lives, we do know something about them. Both sought protection from everything dreadful. Both desired their each and every request to be granted in full. Both hoped for the entire world to experience joy. Both accepted that the buddha's power could satisfy these wishes, and more. Shulkshina and Shulivujna revealed these desires when they had their names copied into incantations at the core of the *Splendid Vision*. As we read in one prayer: "Vajrapani, heed the tathagata's command! Remember your oath! Destroy all disease and every evil! Give us the reward of our choice! May we—Shulkshina and Shulivujna—have each and every request granted in full!" The *Splendid Vision* contains many such pleas.

This sutra belongs to a subgenre of Mahayana Buddhist literature devoted to the ritual worship of books. Like other works associated with the Mahayana book cult, the *Splendid Vision* claims that devotees who offer reverence to the sutra will accumulate a vast hoard of spiritual merit. Again and again, the *Splendid Vision* presents itself as the buddha's present-day equal, worthy of the highest reverence. Yet, whereas one might honor the buddha by offering him robes, food, or a place to dwell, there is no better way to venerate a sutra than to copy it by hand. Thus, the bodhisattva Avalokiteshvara promises that everybody who copies the *Splendid Vision,* or hires somebody else to copy it, will escape the effects of bad karma, whether they are the result of physically harming others or just the intention to do harm. Anyone who copies this sutra, Avalokiteshvara says, will glow with vigor and become wealthy. Who doesn't want to be energetic, happy, rich, and free? How difficult is it to imagine that Shulkshina and Shulivujna created this Sanskrit manuscript of the *Splendid Vision* during the very ritual that Avalokiteshvara enjoins for that act?

The *Splendid Vision* makes extraordinary claims for itself. It promises to answer all prayers, to be a source of wealth, power, and fame, and even to ensure a faithful reader's future buddhahood. Shulkshina and Shulivujna could have asked for no treasure more precious than to hold, read, and study this sutra once again in some future life. Thus, as you read this book, know that according to the *Splendid Vision*'s own inner logic, you yourself might be Shulkshina or Shulivujna reborn, reaping the reward of your previous good deeds.

As for myself, I first encountered the *Splendid Vision* while a graduate student researching female divinities associated with the Ajanta Caves, an ancient Buddhist monastery in western India. My professors at the time urged me to take a deeper interest in the sutra. Eventually this led me to the National Archive in New Delhi, where I reviewed the original Sanskrit birch-bark manuscripts. Then, however, I put the project on the back burner while I pursued other research.

Nearly two decades passed. Although the philological investigation of the *Splendid Vision*'s Sanskrit manuscripts was the original heart of the project, I have elected to publish the fruit of that labor separately.[1] Indeed, over the past decade my own engagement with the study of Buddhism has shifted. In the process of writing my first book, *Beyond Enlightenment: Buddhism, Religion, Modernity*,[2] I came to recognize that the most salient questions for me are not those of the specialist historian about the past contexts of past phenomena but rather the questions of the artist and the activist. How does the past exist for the present? How might one now use representations of the past as means through which to imagine and pursue possible futures?

Here I continue to survey that intellectual terrain. This is not yet another textbook introduction to Mahayana Buddhism or sutra literature. Rather, it is an exploration of the act of reading. It asks how the contingencies, uncertainties, and incompletenesses of the lived present determine our reception of the past. And it tries to answer these complex questions by taking an ancient Indian Mahayana sutra—the *Splendid Vision*—as an exemplum. This book emphasizes dynamic practices of interpretation, rather than the quantifiable accumulation of knowledge about the past, or even truths from the past. It is less concerned with giving you expertise in a distinct subject matter than with giving you a model for how to understand yourself. It recognizes that people do not read books because they cannot think of anything *else* to do but because they cannot think of anything *better* to do. Pick up a Mahayana sutra. Read it. Ponder it. You have just performed a creative act. This book is an exploration of that creativity.

While the approach may be challenging at times, the volume's structure is simple enough. There are four chapters, each clear in purpose. The book begins with an introduction to the *Splendid Vision*. Where does this sutra come from? Why is it worth reading? What sorts of issues does it raise in particular? What principles guide the translation from Sanskrit to English? This introduction is followed by a translation of the sutra itself. The third section forms the intellectual heart of the book. The analytic essay explores how the *Splendid Vision* works as a *scripture*. To elucidate the genre of scripture, the essay presents a heuristic model featuring three generic properties, speaking to concerns for value, truth, and meaning. A mere text becomes a sacred scripture when it has a community that treats it (1) as a receptacle of extraordinary value, (2) as an authoritative source of truth about the cosmos, and (3) as a guide to meaningful action for life. The explanation of the genre of scripture in relation to the *Splendid Vision* progressively unveils how the sutra expresses its own authority, inspires its readers to accept that authority, and promises superior power and accomplishments to those who implement its teachings. Reading scripture is a creative act, on this model, because one cannot do so without participating in practices of self-fashioning and world-fashioning. Finally, the fourth section is a glossary of Sanskrit terms, Indian cultural figures, and Buddhist doctrines found in the sutra.

Anyone who teaches undergraduate courses on a regular basis is bound to be disappointed by lacunae in the available textbooks and sources. I returned to the *Splendid Vision* after having let my transcription of the Sanskrit sit idle for nearly two decades precisely because I wished to fill a gap in my teaching repertoire. As such, I am also aware that sometimes readers and professors are not quite sure how to break up a book, where to locate the conceptual fault lines among the chapters. Here is my advice. If you intend to read the book in two sittings, then focus on the introduction and translation in one session, and the interpretive essay in the second. If you are planning to complete the book in three sittings, first read the introduction and translation; second, read the essay section, "Reading Sutras in Theory and in Practice"; third, finish the essay. The glossary is there to consult whenever you need it.

And speaking of needs, I need to thank the good folk without whom there would be no book. My graduate advisers, Luis Gómez and Walter Spink, set me on course. Now that I have students of my own,

I am always grateful for their friendship and intelligence. In particular, Rachel Gostenhoffer, Stuart Parker, and Devon Pryor helped me to sweeten my words and crystallize my ideas. Rachel and Stuart: deep gratitude! Tom Wall, thank you for asking the right questions at the right time. Likewise, Columbia University Press's anonymous readers offered invaluable guidance for polishing the rough stone of my initial draft.

Twenty years ago I did the philological research that underlies this book. Ten years before that Nancy Caciola came into my life. I expect her to be here thirty years from now as well. And all along the way, I cannot imagine that anything I've done or accomplished would have met with the same success had I lacked her love and support. Yet even before Nancy, there were my parents: Bernice and David Cohen. I dedicate this book to them, with gratitude and love. May every obstacle be removed from their paths. May their every aspiration be realized. Whether they seek happiness, wealth, contentment, or wisdom, may it be theirs.

THE SPLENDID VISION

TRANSLATION

Gilgit's Splendid Vision

The present translation of the *Splendid Vision* is based upon a manuscript of the sutra discovered outside the village of Naupur, near the town of Gilgit, in Pakistan's northern reaches. Located high in the Himalaya Mountains, Gilgit has long been a way station on the Silk Road, along the branch that connects South Asia to central and East Asia, as well as to Europe. One day in 1931, two villagers were grazing cows in a pasture outside Naupur. Idly poking the dirt, one of them discovered several stamped clay tablets. The local people called these earth rupees, money from the earth. Intrigued, he continued digging until he came upon a wooden beam. Fearing that he had uncovered a grave, the cowherd did not dig further. But early the next morning another villager sneaked out, back to the pasture, and shoveled until he found a large wooden chest. Whether he fancied himself a grave robber or treasure hunter, we can feel his great anticipation becoming still greater disappointment as he opened the large chest to reveal four smaller wooden boxes, each of which held, not rubies and coins, but bundles of birch-bark leaves covered with strange black glyphs. An escapade that began with hopes of money from the earth ended with a treasure that, perhaps, only a scholar could love—the Gilgit manuscripts.[1]

Why were those birch-bark leaves buried there in just that way? When the Gilgit manuscripts were first discovered, scholars reconstructed a history as follows: In the middle of the eighth century C.E., the people, perhaps the king, or maybe some monks in Gilgit, sponsored the construction of a large stupa, almost twenty feet wide at its base and forty feet tall. This stupa had two stories inside; the casket with the manuscripts was placed in the upper story, along with clay tablets and perhaps even one or two bronze statues. The manuscripts were sealed up inside the stupa when it was first built. Once interred, these books were never again expected to be read.

Why bury books? Among the likely rationales, scholars found their favorite in the annals of Buddhist doctrine, harking back to the life of Shakyamuni himself. After the Budha died his body was cremated, leaving behind bits of ash and bone. Called *sharira* in Sanskrit, these bodily relics were valued beyond measure. The buddha's followers gathered those *sharira* and put them into memorial shrines called *stupas*. Stupas were public places open to anyone who desired to venerate Shakyamuni; they also served as centers for festivals and pilgrimage. Eventually it came to be believed that the buddha's physical body was not the only source of *sharira*. Even sutras written on birch bark could serve as body doubles for the buddha. Like bodily remains, manuscripts containing the buddha's words could be housed inside stupas, suffusing them with spiritual power. Buddhists called such relics dharma relics. Going back perhaps to the time of Shakyamuni, Buddhists have spoken of the buddha as having a "body of dharma," meaning the corpus of his teachings. Thus, although stupas are best known as monuments containing remains of Shakyamuni's physical body, they could also rightfully house his dharma body, that is, the birchbark leaves conveying his teachings and truths. Indeed, the *Splendid Vision* itself repeats numerous times that everywhere the sutra goes it will perform the same function as a buddha. Presumably, that "everywhere" included a stupa's interior.

Yet, though scholars were long persuaded by this story, none of it is correct. In a recent reevaluation of the archaeological evidence surrounding Gilgit, Gérard Fussman has composed a much more prosaic tale.[2] The Gilgit manuscripts were volumes in the library of an order of Buddhist *acaryas* living in Gilgit. As Buddhist priests, Gilgit's *acaryas* would have made their living by performing rituals and ceremonies on behalf of the local community. The wood beams first noticed by the cowherd were not the superstructure of a stupa in which the buddha's dharma body was interred. Rather, it was the timber frame of the *acaryas'* ancestral home and chapel. The Gilgit manuscripts were the *acaryas'* personal books: inherited books, books they used in their daily vocation, gifts of books from grateful clients. The sutras were buried in rubble when the house collapsed. We do not know why the *acaryas* left their books behind. Might a sudden earthquake have brought the house down? Fussman does not offer a strong opinion for why the *acaryas* abandoned their home. He does propose, however, that the roof collapsed under the weight of the accumulated snow, since no one remained to clear it away.

We have these ancient tracts and treatises, not because pious Buddhists secreted them with sublime expectations inside a mystic tomb, but due to chance factors involving economics, human migration, and most of all, the weather.

The majority of the Gilgit manuscripts came to be housed in the National Archive in New Delhi. The archive's catalog lists sixty-two separate manuscripts, belonging to a variety of Buddhist literary genres.[3] There were disciplinary texts, most notably the *vinaya* of the Mulasarvastivada sect: a compendium of stories, sacred biography, and monastic rules. There were texts that sing praises of the buddha and of the bodhisattva Avalokiteshvara. There were collections of incantations, spells, and prayers. There were some sutras that we might now associate with the so-called Hinayana. There were numerous Mahayana sutras, whose names are familiar to modern students of Buddhism: the *Lotus Sutra*, the *Diamond Sutra*, as well as other sutras on the Perfection of Wisdom. And there were several Mahayana sutras that are not so well known, including the *Splendid Vision*.

Even if the *Splendid Vision* had no other merits, it could still lay claim to having the longest title among all the manuscripts discovered at Gilgit: *Sarvatathagatadhishthana-satvavalokana-buddhakshet-*

rasandarshana-vyuha.[4] However, the sutra does have other points of interest, first among which is that the *Splendid Vision* was translated into the Chinese and Tibetan languages. These translations, in turn, point toward a curious textual history.

Gilgit's version of the *Splendid Vision* is composed of a series of six formulaic monologues. In each monologue, the speaker recites a mantra, a collection of words and sounds that are believed to possess innate power. Each then describes a ritual through which to harness the mantra's power and make it effective. Each, finally, describes a series of benefits and blessings that will accrue to all who recite the mantra and perform the liturgy. Interspersed among these monologues are cries of excitement and approval, lamentations about the evil state of the world, and assertions of the sutra's cosmic importance. The *Splendid Vision* was translated into Tibetan based upon a version rather close to that buried in Gilgit. This Tibetan translation was made by Yeshe De, a prolific translator working in the early 800s. The Chinese translation dates to approximately one hundred years earlier and was produced by Yijing, a celebrated pilgrim from China to India. Yijing left his homeland in 671 and returned in 695, carrying a collection of over four hundred Indian texts, one of which was the *Splendid Vision*. Yijing's version of the *Splendid Vision* was significantly shorter than both the Gilgit manuscript and the Tibetan.

In sum, there are three extant manuscript traditions for the *Splendid Vision*, each approximately one century apart. The earliest existing manuscript, from Gilgit, has six monologues. The next oldest manuscript tradition was brought from India's Gangetic basin to China, and it has only one monologue. The most recent of the three, known through the Tibetan translation, is similar in length and structure to the first. Thus, the *Splendid Vision*'s three manuscript traditions fit into two separate lines of descent. The Gilgit and Tibetan versions belong together; the Chinese version was translated from a considerably different Sanskrit original.[5]

There is one more interesting, perhaps even crucial, note to be made about the specific manuscript upon which the following translation is based. That manuscript contains the names of two people: a man, Shulkshina, and a woman, Shulivujna. These names are found inserted in the mantras and incantations that, when recited, are supposed to protect and serve the person who recites the mantra. The inclusion of these names suggests that this particular manuscript of the *Splendid Vision* had the explicit purpose of freeing Shulkshina and Shulivujna from suffering. Unfortunately, this manuscript does not also include a colophon, an afterword to the text, naming the people who sponsored the manuscript's production and explaining why they undertook that act. So, we cannot be sure whether Shulkshina and Shulivujna themselves sponsored the transcription of this sutra, or whether they were the beneficiaries of some other patron's largesse.

We also are not quite sure where Shulkshina and Shulivujna came from. Oskar von Hinüber, who has made an extensive investigation into these two people's names and titles as recorded in the *Splendid Vision*, found elements that he associated with the Chinese, Iranian, Sogdian, Sakan, and Sanskrit languages.[6] The apparent internationalism of these names and titles is fitting, for Gilgit was an important way station on trans-Himalayan caravan routes at the time. Indeed, Gilgit and the nearby town of Chilas are littered with ancient graffiti, attesting to a nonstop circulation of Buddhist pilgrims, monks, and traders through this mountainous region throughout the period from the fifth through the eighth centuries. Yet our knowledge remains tantalizingly incomplete. We do not know the homeland of Shulkshina and Shulivujna, or whether they themselves were even responsible for the production of this manuscript. They may have been the parents of the manuscript's sponsor(s). Those sponsor(s) may have been travelers who decided to have a transcription of the *Splendid Vision* made for protection before they crossed the high ridge that locals called the Snow Mountains.

Sutra as Readymade: A Rationale for Reading

The mere fact that somebody imagined the *Splendid Vision* could protect Shulkshina and Shulivujna from suffering does not necessarily make it worthwhile to read. In the big picture, the *Splendid Vision* is insignificant. Yes, some people thought it was worth copying and storing in a box, while others gave their time to translate it for Chinese and Tibetan devotees. Yet beyond these thin truths, we cannot say much. No supplementary records describe the *Splendid Vision*'s role in the life of a community of Buddhists. No external chronicles document whether the sutra was read or recited, or whether its rituals were enacted as prescribed, on the eighth day of the waxing moon. Buddhist scholastics of the era did not cite the *Splendid Vision* as a proof text for their ideas. And in general there is no evidence that the *Splendid Vision* ever made a palpable or noteworthy contribution to the advancement of Buddhism in any land. Even modern scholars have not written much about it.

So why should one read this sutra, or indeed read about it? A cultural critic, Pierre Bourdieu, points toward an answer when he observes

> There is nothing more difficult to convey than reality in all its ordinariness. Flaubert was fond of saying that it takes a lot of hard work to portray mediocrity. Sociologists run into this problem all the time: How can we make the ordinary extraordinary and evoke ordinariness in such a way that people will see just how extraordinary it is?[7]

Yes, there is an extraordinary wealth of insight to be gained from the *Splendid Vision* . . . if we mine it for its thin truths, its mediocrities.

In light of Bourdieu's words, consider the curious case of the Gilgit manuscripts' reception by scholars. While the dominant discourse held that these texts were intentionally buried in a stupa, beginning with the earliest published reports, in fact scholars were not sure whether the wooden beams belonged to a stupa or some other kind of building. Likewise, they were not sure whether the cache of manuscripts was the enshrined dharma body of a buddha or a library hidden, perhaps, from an invading army. Yet prior to Fussman's recent article, although scholars did tell several different stories about the Gilgit manuscripts, their diverse interpretations shared one basic assumption: the preservation of the Gilgit manuscripts was somehow a direct consequence of the texts' spiritual function. Or to recollect Bourdieu, scholars sought extraordinary reasons for how and why this extraordinary cache of manuscripts survived intact for an extraordinary length of time. And they found those extraordinary reasons in the arcana of Buddhist doctrine and ritual. What did Fussman do differently? He took a cold eye to all this Buddhist heat. He did not allow a scholarly passion for Buddhism to color how he saw the naked facts. In all ordinariness: It snowed. The roof collapsed. The books survived. How ordinary the circumstances and yet also how extraordinary the result.

Scholars are not well equipped to deal with ordinariness. We make our living by observing subtle distinctions and nuanced truths. We make our reputation by explaining anomalies. We make intellectual love to the exception and the exceptional. Artists have it easier. Like Marcel Duchamp, when artists walk, the mere rubbing of their corduroy trousers becomes music to their ears.[8] As a work of Buddhist literature, the *Splendid Vision* is much like Duchamp's corduroy trousers. To hear its potent trivialities as music, we must listen with artists' ears. Indeed, to learn the trick, let us delve deeper into the work of Marcel Duchamp, one of the twentieth century's most innovative and influential artists. Let us consider Duchamp's theory of found art.

In 1917, Duchamp, using the pseudonym Richard Mutt, submitted a work entitled *Fountain* to the New York Independent Artists Exhibition. The work was accepted into the exhibition sight unseen. But once the exhibition committee actually saw *Fountain*, they quickly hid the object from public view. The committee was scandalized, for *Fountain* was nothing other than a porcelain urinal that Duchamp had salvaged, turned on its back, signed, dated, and placed on a pedestal.

Ordinarily a urinal is a place for quick relief. Set on a pedestal, given a title, signed, and exhibited, that urinal becomes a fountain, extraordinary. Duchamp's point—one that still meets controversy—was that craft and technical skill are not needed for great art. The most ordinary (for a man, at least) and mediocre object can become art if treated skillfully with imagination, intellect, and will. To this day,

Fountain remains a stirring high point in the history of modernism. If an artist can take a mundane object usually hidden behind locked doors and, by calling it *Fountain*, actually transform it into a fountain suitable for public view, then art is not a matter of aesthetics or beauty: art emerges out of the artist's creative appropriation of authority. If a urinal can become a fountain, what cannot be thus transformed? Duchamp's *Fountain* raises these questions: If anything can be presented as a work of art, then is "ordinariness" not simply a matter of perspective? Is not the same true of "extraordinariness"? Was Duchamp saying, piss on art? Or, piss has an aesthetic quality all its own? Or simply, drink piss?

Duchamp characterized *Fountain* as a *readymade*, a found object. The *Splendid Vision*, too, is something of a readymade. Translated into English, the *Splendid Vision* comes to you processed, complete, accessible, present. You receive it as a manufactured object without (so I am guessing) paying any mind to the thousands of man-hours or innumerable editors, ink manufacturers, press operators, computer programmers, janitors, and farmers who were instrumental in bringing it to your eyes. And like a urinal, once the thing is in your hands, you know what to do with it, and where, for the book's front cover clads the *Splendid Vision* in the vitreous porcelain of Buddhist scripture.

The challenge of the readymade is to hear music in the rustling of corduroy or to appreciate a toilet as a fountain. But the challenge works in both directions. Duchamp, for instance, mused about using a canvas of Rembrandt's as an ironing board. Art is also needed to appreciate the mundanities of that which seems so very special. We do not affix urinals to the walls of our kitchens and classrooms. Though common objects, they are hidden objects, secreted behind locked doors. *Fountain* falls into a curious interpretive limbo, betwixt and between. So too the *Splendid Vision*: though commonplace as a book and generic as a scripture, this narrative contains many marvels. Readers of the sutra meet superhuman beings who are capable of bending space and time to their wills, who speak words that make all dreams come true. Duchamp's artistry challenges us to appreciate the *Splendid Vision*'s amazements as culturally specific expressions of dirt-ordinary human concerns. From this perspective, the sutra is special precisely because there is little special about it. The *Splendid Vision* is valuable precisely because it so readily conveys the strangeness of India's past in all its normalcy, opening a wide window onto the everyday character of value, truth, meaning in that day and in ours.

Before we move on to the translation of the *Splendid Vision*, Duchamp's *Fountain* can reveal still another dimension of this sutra as a found object. Although Duchamp might have intended *Fountain* to demonstrate the far reaches of the individual artist's autonomy, he demonstrated, in fact, the tensions between creative authorship and institutional authority. *Fountain* was not hailed as art when it was first presented. To the contrary, Duchamp's work was nearly rejected and ejected from the 1917 exhibition before the show had opened—even though the show was not juried, and even though participants were supposed to be allowed to display whatever they wished. In order to keep *Fountain* out, the exhibition's curators broke their own rules. (What's more ordinary that that?) Duchamp's contemporaries were not reacting simply to the unwelcome presence of a urinal on a pedestal. More shocking yet was Duchamp's thumb-biting arrogance. For, he sought to authorize his work as art by appropriating the same conventions that other, "legitimate," artists use to authorize themselves: a title, a signature, a date, an exhibition. Lacking these institutional props, *Fountain* was just a urinal, and not even a working one at that.[9] Institutions organize themselves around conventions and preserve their identities by policing those conventions. In turn, the successful appropriation of acknowledged social conventions casts the glamour of authority. It can transform a shockingly new production into a work that is accepted as natural and right. In the long run, Duchamp was successful. Today, if somebody were to put a urinal on exhibit, we would yawn and ask, so what?

And so, just as Duchamp challenges us to consider the *Splendid Vision*'s prodigies and portents in all their human ordinariness, his art also sheds light on the social inflections of our own contemporary intellectual practices. You have opened this book and are making the effort to confront its strangeness because you are on a unique quest: to broaden your knowledge, to fathom your heritage, to find inspiration for your own art, to get a good grade in a class. For you to be able to accept this book as appropriate for the task, it must present the *Splendid Vision* in a way that satisfies your conventionalized expectations. Thus, although I produced a free, colloquial translation of the sutra, I nevertheless felt it necessary to also include an extensive glossary, an exegetical essay, as well as reference to my publication of the Sanskrit manuscripts, all with the express purpose of bolstering the authority of this volume and appropriating the authorizing capacity of institutional academia as my own.

In turn, we can recursively bring this perspective back to the *Splendid Vision* itself. The Gilgit manuscripts would seem to disclose the actual beliefs, hopes, dreams, and ideals held by the community of Buddhists living near Gilgit. However, some appearances are deceiving, and some are not. As you read the translation, consider that the *Splendid Vision*, like *Fountain*, may be a skillful pretense, playing on its ancient audience's expectations. This sutra may not reflect actual, lived belief at the time of its creation but may instead be a simulacrum of lived belief: a representation of dharma as its author would have liked it to be seen, known, and lived. As a perfectly ordinary human product, it may dissimulate in its abstractions, even if it cannot lie in its naked form. We do not know. Duchamp's *Fountain* transformed the ordinary into the extraordinary by appropriating and twisting conventional expectations about art and authority. We should learn its lesson and be aware that the *Splendid Vision* may likewise appropriate and twist institutional norms in order to authorize its own beliefs, hopes, dreams, and ideals. We do not want to be like an art historian who, millennia from now, discovers a photograph of *Fountain* and writes a scholarly treatise on the early twentieth-century fad for drinking water from urinals.

How does the *Splendid Vision* establish its own authority? The sutra appeals to institutional conventions in relation to concerns for value, truth, and meaning. Is this reliance on authority, in fact, what is so ordinary about the text? Keep these questions in mind as you read the *Splendid Vision*'s translation. We shall return to them in the interpretive essay that follows.

Regarding the Translation

"Rules," writes Vatsyayana, author of the *Kama Sutra*, "are a necessary prerequisite, even if one strays from them."[10] That which Vatsyayana claims here for love and sex holds true for translation as well. One cannot move meaning between two languages without a clear set of principles to guide that work.

Given my interpretive focus on the ordinary and everyday, I set out to create a translation that is accessible to a general readership and makes sense in English, rather than one that preserves the Sanskrit's every grammatical particularity and terminological nuance. To accomplish this, my technique was straightforward, if not simple. First, I made a literal, technically accurate translation, adhering closely to the manuscript's syntax and vocabulary. Properly speaking, this was not so much a translation as a rendering into a Sanskrit-English hybrid, a language readily comprehensible to professional scholars of Buddhism and opaque to all normal readers. Then I reworked sentence structures, adjusted numbers (single to plural, or vice versa), shifted word orders, and replaced terse technical terminologies with elucidatory paraphrases—without looking at the Sanskrit—until I removed much of the first draft's hybridity and fustiness. Next, I checked my work against the Sanskrit, to make sure that I had not strayed from the original *too* egregiously. Finally, I further crafted the English. Vatsyayana would be proud: these were my rules and I did stray from them now and then.

The Sanskrit manuscripts of the *Splendid Vision* were composed in a dialect of Sanskrit that does not respect the grammatical precision of the classical language. The *Splendid Vision*'s hybrid Sanskrit is a grammatical hodgepodge, mixing singular and plural numbers, past and present tenses, male, female, and neuter genders. The translation should show no evidence of this grammatical mess. Similarly, the Sanskrit includes long constructions, unwieldy phrases, and plodding lists. I have shortened, tightened, and straightened these syntactic elements in keeping with the standards of clear English prose.

Moreover, in the interest of enhancing the translation's ordinariness and accessibility, I have avoided much of the apparatus common to technical treatments of Buddhist texts. The translation does not mark paraphrases or interpolations by placing them in brackets. Likewise it does not explain my difficulties with the manuscript through linguistic or philological notes. In one case, for instance, the Sanskrit is ambiguous as to whether it is discussing a mantra or the entire sutra. In another case, the author wrote 800 (*aṣṭa śata*) in a context for which all other parallel instances have 108 (*aṣṭaśata*). In such instances, I made an interpretive choice, which I do not mark as such. This is meant to be a work in English. The exotica of Sanskrit graphical conventions and lexical difficulties should not obstruct the reader's access to the exotica of the sutra's expressions of scripturality, authority, and power. As I noted earlier, individuals who have the skills and interest to consider the buddhological and philological details of this sutra can consult transcriptions of the original manuscripts and form their own theories therefrom. The manuscripts are problematic and those who wish to quibble with my choices will find themselves in a hermeneuticist's heaven.

Of course, even though I have sought to make this text's language relatively transparent to a contemporary reader, full transparency is undesirable, let alone impossible. Several terms have been left untranslated, either because they have entered into English (e.g., bodhisattva, mantra), or because they are so complex or rich in nuance that a gloss is insufficient (e.g., bali, yakshini). I have included a glossary to explain these untranslated words as well as to clarify important Sanskrit terms that I did gloss or paraphrase in the body of the translation. Glossary items appear in boldface at their first occurrence in the book.

Moreover, all section titles and paragraph numbers in the translation are my additions.

Finally, please note that the Gilgit manuscript of the *Splendid Vision* is incomplete. In order to provide a full translation of the sutra, I relied on the Tibetan version for my translation into English of section numbers 1 through 12, inclusive.[11]

TRANSLATION

The Assembly

1   Thus have I heard. At one time the **blessed lord** was staying at the home of noble **Avalokiteshvara** on **Potalaka Mountain**.

2   Seated on a divine lion throne, encrusted with priceless jewels and strewn with flowers, the blessed lord was surrounded by a grand assembly of monks, numbering five hundred monks. These monks were all **arhats** who had dried up the **sources from which karma streams forth**. Each one had attained the supreme perfection of total control over his own thoughts.

3   As for the **bodhisattvas** present: All were firm in their knowledge of **great compassion**. All were bound for one more birth, or two births, or three births, or ten births, or twenty births, or thirty births, or one hundred births. All had reached either the eighth or tenth **stage on the bodhisattva path** to buddhahood. Seven hundred **bodhisattva mahasattvas** were present, including noble Avalokiteshvara, **Manjushri**, Vimalaketu, Ratnashri, Vajraketu, Vimalaprabha, Candrana, and Amritaketu.

4   Every layman and laywoman present had received a **prophecy that he or she would become a buddha**. All had attained states of **samadhi**. Gathered from various **world systems**, they numbered five thousand.

5   The blessed lord was also accompanied by one hundred thousand **gods**, **nagas**, **yakshas**, and **gandharvas**, all of whom had wor-

shiped past buddhas and had seen **tathagatas** perform extraordinary marvels.

6 The great **yakshinis** also were present. All these yakshinis possessed knowledge proper to a bodhisattva. Each had received a prophecy that she would become a buddha. They were assured that they would **never stop progressing toward buddhahood**. There were eighty great yakshinis, including **Anopama**, Vimalaprabha, Prabhavati, **Bhima**, Shri, Hariti, and **Shankhini**.

7 All the world's guardians were also there with the blessed lord, including **Indra** and **Brahma**, the **four great kings**, as well as Manibhadra and Purnabhadra, generals in the yaksha army.

8 Then, seeing the tathagata seated on the lion throne, they all worshiped and venerated him—each according to his own **roots of virtue**—with celestial ornaments, clothes, flowers, garlands, incense, balms, and the sounds of musical instruments. Several circumambulated the tathagata many hundreds of thousands of times in his honor.

Setting the Scene

9 Then, at that time, the blessed lord entered into a samadhi named *abiding in the knowledge of great compassion, which takes all beings as its object of contemplation.* Through the power of that samadhi, this **universe of three-thousand many-thousand worlds** was filled with light. Once the whole universe was aglow, the blind could see. The deaf could hear. The sick became healthy. The naked were clothed. The mad gained their sanity. Beings whose bodies had withered and whose senses had dulled found their bodies and senses restored. The poor became wealthy. Those who didn't have wealth, property, or pleasures came to possess wealth, property, and pleasures. Everybody was full of joy and their hopes were totally fulfilled.

10 Inspired, every living being in this universe of three-thousand many-thousand worlds approached the blessed lord to hear the dharma. All who had been born as gods forgot their divine plea-

sures and turned their attention to the buddha. They then went to the blessed lord in order to hear the dharma. Likewise, all who had been born human forgot their human pleasures and went to the blessed lord in order to hear the dharma. Likewise, all born as nagas, yakshas, **wild demons**, **hungry ghosts**, and **haunting ghouls** also turned their attention to the buddha. They became full of benevolence for all living things. At ease in body and mind, they approached the blessed lord in order to hear the dharma. Through the buddha's power, even beings born in the thick gloom of **Yama's realm** received vision for a single moment, became aware of one another, and were released from that great darkness. All living beings came to love one another and were freed of emotional torment.

11 Then, at that time, the earth shook in six directions, rising and falling.

12 Then princely Manjushri joined the congregation. He sat down and said this to noble Avalokiteshvara, the bodhisattva mahasattva, "**Son of good family**, I see a large congregation of bodhisattvas and recognize the omen of a grand assembly. Son of good family, I see many hundreds of thousands of millions of bodhisattvas who have heard prophecies of their own future buddhahood[1] and recognize the omen of a momentous discourse on dharma: a discourse that will fulfill the hopes of many hundreds of thousands of millions of beings, who will gain great knowledge. This being the case, son of good family, stir your compassion for living beings. To benefit them, to make them happy, and still more, to help them attain **unsurpassed, complete, and perfect awakening**, question the tathagata!

13 "**In the last time, in the last period**, there will be people who will do bad things. They will be poor and oppressed. They will have sickly complexions. Old age and disease will weigh heavily upon them. They will have few possessions. Their bodies will lack vitality. They will die young. They will lack intelligence. Lust,

hatred, and delusion will crush them. For their sake, son of good family, beg the tathagata to teach the dharma! Do it for their continuing benefit and happiness! Do it to alleviate all sickness! Do it to keep them from evil! Do it to stop their evil! Do it to fulfill all their hopes! And to end the list: do it so that they might attain **supreme final nirvana!**"

14 Then noble Avalokiteshvara, the bodhisattva mahasattva, looked out to the **ten directions**, calling to mind tens of millions of tathagatas, as numerous as the sands of the Ganges River. Avalokiteshvara saluted the buddha with folded hands, circled him three times, and prostrated flat on the ground.

15 He said, "Blessed lord, in the last time there will be people tormented by old age, disease, sorrow, mortality, calamities, or an untimely death. They will be oppressed. They will have sickly complexions. They will die young. They will have few possessions. Their bodies will lack vitality. Jealous, immoral thoughts will push them to kill each other. They will steal each other's wealth, possessions, and power. They will revel in frivolities, like laughing, dancing, and performances. They will **mistakenly perceive permanence in the impermanent**. They will mistakenly find purity in the impure.

16 "From these causes, for these reasons, because these people will have done harm in so many ways, they will be reborn in the hells, among the animals, or in Yama's realm. Blessed lord, I am concerned for these beings. I wish them well and want all their hopes to be realized. The list goes on and on, but to conclude: I hope to spread the tathagata's knowledge, to enable beings to be reborn in **buddhafields**, and to bring all evil to an end. Thus, I implore: Speak, blessed lord! Speak, **sugata**! There is no truth that the tathagata has not understood, seen, heard, or realized. Blessed lord, many bodhisattvas, monks, nuns, laymen, laywomen, gods, and nagas have gathered here, wanting to hear dharma teachings. They have served previous buddhas and are wise. Let them not be disappointed!"

17 Then that entire assembly prostrated on the ground. With one voice they shouted, "Excellent, blessed lord! Please speak, blessed lord! Please speak, sugata!"

Shakyamuni's Discourse

18 Then the blessed lord considered their request for a second and third time. Looking out to the ten directions, he answered noble Avalokiteshvara, the bodhisattva mahasattva, with a sweet and captivating voice.

19 "Son of good family, there is a samadhi named *the splendid vision in which one observes living beings and reveals buddhafields through the empowerment of all tathagatas.* I learned this samadhi from the tathagata Sukusumajyotihsandarshana in the past, when I first conceived the **aspiration to awaken as a buddha**. Just by hearing this samadhi's name, nine hundred million beings attained the knowledge of the tathagatas. Tathagatas in many different buddhafields foretold that every one of them would attain buddhahood. I received a prophecy too. I recollect this, son of good family, through a tathagata's divine knowledge.

20 "Thirty thousand tathagatas have already preached this dharma discourse in order to benefit living beings. Every time, noble Avalokiteshvara, you asked the tathagata to speak. Likewise, an organized congregation of bodhisattvas, monks, nuns, laymen, and laywomen, as well as princely Manjushri, witnessed the dharma discourse and performed acts of reverence and worship.

21 "In this way, many hundreds of thousands of millions of living beings received prophecies that they would become buddhas in the future. They attained the samadhis of a bodhisattva. Their every desire was satisfied and their every hope fulfilled. They became free of disease. They brought past good deeds to fruition. They eliminated all **obstacles to spiritual progress**. They became congenial, gracious, and attractive. They enriched their treasuries and storerooms with money and grain. They gained favor with

kings, royal advisers, and government ministers. Mindful and wise, they were revered by all living beings. They gained unwavering faith in the buddha, dharma, and sangha. They became content. They became long-lived, attractive, sharp, strong, and vigorous. They became endowed with all the best qualities. Never again were they separated from their loved ones; nor did their dear ones ever suffer misfortune.

22 "Just so, the sons and daughters of good family here today will also come to possess many good qualities, if they act as follows: First, they should prostrate before this dharma discourse, their bodies flat to the ground. Then, they should adorn the dharma discourse with flowers, incense, perfume, garlands, balms, parasols, banners, and flags. Then, they should take refuge in the buddha. After this, they should praise the dharma discourse, concentrate on it, recite it and have others recite it, copy it and have others copy it, with feelings of profound reverence for the **dharma preacher**.

23 "Then, even in this very lifetime, these sons and daughters of good family will come to possess all good qualities. They will become congenial, gracious, and attractive. They will enjoy healthy and long lives. They will become firm in intelligence, mindful, and content. Everybody—kings, queens, princes, government officials, even enemies—will find them worthy of praise, worthy of reverence, worthy of honor. They will act as great philanthropists. The scent of sandalwood will waft from their mouths. Their eyes will be like blue lotuses.

24 "Day and night, they will receive visions of buddhas and bodhisattvas. Every obstacle to spiritual progress will be swept from their paths. Even if they commit evil deeds—including the **five atrocities that have immediate consequences**—the gods will still protect them. At the time of their deaths, they will receive visions of buddhas and bodhisattvas. When they die, their minds will be neither spiteful nor distracted. After their deaths, they will be reborn in the **Land of Bliss**.

25 "These sons and daughters of good family were in my direct presence when I predicted that they would become buddhas. They have seen me, honored me, and revered me. They must have no doubt concerning their own future awakening. Whosoever will preserve this dharma discourse, honor it, copy it and inspire others to copy it, worship it, accept it, and make its name known should be considered a true bodhisattva and honored as such.

26 "There may be individuals who, due to the effects of previous karma, are crippled or miserable or stupid or publically reviled or separated from their loved ones or harassed by the government. The power of this samadhi—just hearing it—will eliminate every bit of karma that impedes their spiritual growth. For some, karmic residues will be removed through the experience of headaches; for some through fasting; for some by wearing rags; for some by having to undergo physical and mental duress; for some through difficulty sleeping; for some through social censure. Thus they should think to themselves: 'Previously, while circling around in samsara, I piled up all sorts of evil misdeeds against living beings. I confess that. I acknowledge it. I do not conceal it.' They should have unwavering faith in the buddha, dharma, and sangha.

27 "Any karma that would result in a son or daughter of good family's becoming destitute, as well as any karma their parents may have accumulated by harming the buddha, dharma, sangha, **disciples**, or **solitary buddhas**—all that karma will be eliminated. So great is this samadhi's majesty!

28 "Likewise, any karmic residue that may be likened to an inferno of pain because it causes a son or daughter of good family to be separated from loved ones, or to be born blind, or as a woman or hermaphrodite, or, through the power of envy, selfishness, and anger, to be reborn in Yama's realm, the realm of hungry ghosts, or that of animals—every such obstacle to spiritual progress will be removed. Thus this samadhi is the source of all good qualities.

29 "Son of good family, there is a reason that this dharma discourse has survived so long. Namely, it contains a **mantra**, an **incanta-**

tion. The words of this mantra guard, protect, and defend sons and daughters of good family. They fulfill all hopes for everything good. They bring the happiness that comes with many possessions and great power. They make all fantasies and wishes come true. They exhaust all karma. They allay nightmares about an early death. They end all disease. They give victory in every battle. They increase longevity, beauty, strength, vigor, and fortitude. They enable one to control all yakshas and ghosts, human beings and **monsters**. They cause all fevers, poisons, fires, and floods to abate. And the list goes on, culminating in the fact that they enable one to receive a prophecy of future buddhahood. After hearing, memorizing, reciting, writing, and inciting others to write this mantra, sons and daughters of good family will obtain all these amazing benefits, even if they act solely out of a desire for self-protection."

30 Then, at that time, the earth quaked in six directions. Members of that well-organized congregation draped the tathagata with flowers, incense, perfume, garlands, and bolts of cotton cloth, shouting their approval, "Excellent, excellent, blessed lord! What is the mantra?"

31 *Homage to all tathagatas! Here is the mantra: Awakened! Well awakened! Awakened mind! Of the world! Apart from the world! Utterly beyond the world! Looking down upon living beings! Empowered with the power of all tathagatas! Fulfiller of wishes! Resplendent! Worshiped by men and gods! Giver of the tathagata's knowledge! By the power of the tathagatas: May the entire world be joyful! May previous karma be removed! May I—**nam-tse hammarapati shulkshina aysadika mahashraddhopasika shulivujna**—be protected from every horror! By the power of the tathagatas! SVAHA*

32 "Hey, son of good family! This is the mantra. Thirty thousand tathagatas have recited it and empowered it. Right now, I too have spoken this mantra, this cure-all, in order to increase the benefit, welfare, and happiness of all beings; in order to guard, protect,

and defend all beings; in order that living beings are reborn in buddhafields.

33 "Suppose someone from the assembly were to wonder, 'How might I acquire all those good qualities about which the tathagata has spoken?' First, he should arise at dawn. Keeping his mind sympathetic, compassionate, and loving toward all living beings, and without any trace of envy, pride, cruelty, or anger, he should concentrate with one-pointed intensity. When his mind is thus composed, he should then perform the **exalted rite** for the buddha. After that, he should pay homage to all tathagatas in the ten directions. Next, he should set his mind upon the object of his desire and intone the mantra 108 times. Finally, he should offer flowers to the tathagata, one flower at a time.

34 "Thereupon, his hopes will be entirely fulfilled. Tathagatas will reveal themselves to him in dreams. Whatever reward he asks for, he will receive. At the time of death, tathagatas will show themselves to him. After death, he will be reborn in the Land of Bliss. He will enjoy a long life, strength, physical beauty, and vigor. He will completely dominate his enemies."

35 Indeed truly, while this incantation was being recited, sixty thousand living beings became **receptive to the truth that phenomena neither come into existence nor cease to exist**. Every obstacle that might have prevented their spiritual progress was eliminated. Every aspiration was realized.

Vajrapani's Discourse

36 After that, the bodhisattva **Vajrapani** looked out to the ten directions and said this to the blessed lord, "There is an incantation named *fearless splendor*—a bodhisattva vow I swore in the presence of the tathagata Abhayavyuharaja and subsequently shared with all living beings. From that day forward, blessed lord, I know of nobody who has heard that incantation, even if it fell into his ear by chance, who has been injured, harmed, or killed through

any of the following causes: physical weakness, affliction, disease, fever, bodily pain, mental duress, early death, flooding, weapons, poison, toxic beverages, **dakinis**, ghosts, yakshas, enemies, humans, or monsters. That simply has not happened.

37 "Therefore, blessed lord, please allow me to share this manifestation of my vow as a bodhisattva, which I offer for the benefit of dharma preachers and dharma students. It fulfills all the hopes of anybody who hears, esteems, worships, preserves, and recites it."

38 *Homage to all buddhas! Homage to all bodhisattvas and arhats! Here is the mantra: OM **Vajra** holder! Vajra holder! Vajra body! Vajra power! Vajra fire! HUM HUM Vajrapani, obey the tathagata's command! Remember your promise! Destroy every sickness and every evil! Give me the gift of my choice! Whatsoever I request, may that be given to me—nam-tse hammarapati shulkshina aysadika shulivujna—in full! HE HE Save! Save! Come! Come! Please do not delay! Show your vajra body! By the power of the tathagatas! SVAHA*

39 While this incantation was being recited, the earth rose up and sank down. The yakshas and wild demons were all confused; while all varieties of beings, from the gods through humans and monsters, were astonished. They shouted their approval. "Excellent, excellent, O great one! The incantation you have recited, the mantra, is supremely powerful."

40 Then the bodhisattva Vajrapani addressed the blessed lord, "Suppose someone truly aspires to ascend the stages of the bodhisattva path. Or maybe he wants wealth, grain, possessions, and power. Or maybe to be a king. Or maybe to be a **sorcerer**. Or maybe health, strength, vigor, and longevity. On the eighth day of the half month when the moon is waxing, that person should carve white sandalwood into the image of **Vajradhara** [i.e., Vajrapani], laughing a horselaugh, adorned with many ornaments. The statue should contain a **relic**. Then after he purifies himself by fasting a day and a night, he should burn incense to this reliquary image of

Vajrapani, the sorcerer and giver of comfort. Moreover, from the eighth day of the half month until the fifteenth day, he should perform the following rite: After he finishes the preparatory service, he should perform a **puja** with ample incense, flowers, perfume, and lamps in a place made sacred by the presence of the tathagata. Next, he should recite the incantation in three sets of 108 repetitions each. He should also perform a puja to the tathagata. Then, after he pays homage to all tathagatas, and after he sets up four full jars, he should construct a **mandala** out of red sandalwood. Then, after dressing himself in white garments and focusing his mind intensely, he should cast a **bali** offering of tasty liquor and fragrant **milk-rice** to the four directions. Lastly, he should strike the Vajrapani with 108 jasmine blossoms.

41 "When this is done, there will be a great roar; the earth will shake; rays of light will shoot forth. Then I will give the desired reward. Just by reciting this incantation, he will be successful in everything he does, whether done by choice or by obligation. He will be free of disease and live a long life. Everything evil will leave him alone. He will come to possess thousands of good qualities. At the time of death, he will see the buddha. I will give a vision of myself as well."

42 The blessed lord then spoke his approval, "Excellent, excellent, Vajrapani! Nothing surpasses this sign of your bodhisattva vow. About that, the world, together with its gods, should harbor neither anxiety, nor disagreement, nor doubt."

Manjushri's Questions—Shakyamuni's Answers

43 After that, princely Manjushri asked the blessed lord, "Why is this samadhi named *the splendid vision in which one observes living beings and reveals buddhafields through the empowerment of all tathagatas?*"

44 The blessed lord replied, "Someone empowered through the empowerment of all tathagatas and all bodhisattvas attains every

samadhi and access to every incantation. He discerns the **inner flow of the minds and mental factors** of all beings—gods, nagas, humans, yakshas, gandharvas, hungry ghosts, animals, and the inhabitants of Yama's realm. Thus he is able to distinguish spiritually meritorious beings, who do good deeds and gain faith in the **three jewels**, from evildoers destined for hell and hard labor. Knowing this, he teaches dharma to those who adopt evil views. He restrains them from all immorality, laying a foundation for them to awaken as buddhas. He satisfies their every desire, removing any reason for them to feel envy, pride, anger, or selfishness. In turn, they also gain faith in the three jewels and are reborn in buddhafields. Never again will they experience misery or melancholy. Son of good family, this is why this samadhi is named *the splendid vision in which one observes living beings and reveals buddhafields through the empowerment of all tathagatas.* After hearing it, living beings definitely attain the stage on the bodhisattva path at which they are assured that they will never stop progressing toward buddhahood."

45 Manjushri then asked, "Blessed lord, how do sons of good family receive a prophecy regarding their own future buddhahood? How much **spiritual merit** must they accumulate? What sort of difficult tasks must they perform? Blessed lord, attaining arhatship is hard work. How much more difficult must it be to attain unsurpassed, complete, and perfect awakening!"

46 The blessed lord replied, "Son of good family, starting with my initial aspiration for buddhahood, I accumulated spiritual merit as I perfected the **bodhisattva's perfections** of giving, morality, patience, vigor, meditation, and wisdom. I also accumulated spiritual merit by giving away my head, hands, feet, eyes, torso, as well as my beloved sons, wives, daughters, male and female slaves. So too, one accumulates spiritual merit by worshiping, honoring, reciting, learning, copying, and having others copy this dharma discourse. One accumulates spiritual merit by sharing this dharma discourse with others. And one accumulates spiritual merit

by worshiping and honoring dharma-preachers who preach this discourse. The volume of merit I amassed through a bodhisattva's perfections and heroic self-sacrifice does not approach even the hundredth part of the latter quantities, amassed by virtue of this dharma discourse.

47 "Furthermore, son of good family, suppose someone were to honor, revere, esteem, and worship all the dharma that I previously taught and mastered. Suppose that, after he honors all this dharma, he then copies it or has others copy it. By contrast, if somebody else were to take this particular dharma discourse and copy, recite, worship, and disseminate it, he would lay hold of a greater accumulation of spiritual merit than that.

48 "Thus the tathagata prophesies that he will attain unsurpassed, complete, and perfect awakening. Why? Because it is difficult for evildoers to hear, learn, remember, worship, and copy a dharma discourse such as this. It is difficult for people who delight in eating, drinking, joking, and dancing. It is difficult for people who mistakenly find purity in the impure. It is difficult for people bursting with lust, anger, and hatred. It is difficult for people who mistakenly find satisfaction in the unsatisfactory. It is difficult for people who delight in arguments, curses, threats, and fights. Such people will not understand this dharma discourse, nor will they sharpen their minds.

49 "Accordingly, they do not know the consequences of evil deeds. Bad friends surround them. Old age, disease, sorrow, and death oppress them. For them, the moment of death is a horror. Although they see each other being laid out on biers ready for the charnel ground, they do not conceive meritorious thoughts or unwavering faith. So after death, they suffer misery again and again.

50 "Son of good family, if somebody has not planted any roots of virtue, or has not seen a tathagata, or has not received a prophecy of future buddhahood, then he will fail to hear this dharma discourse. Likewise, he will fail to respect, worship, learn, copy, have

copied, or place his faith in it. He will also fail to honor, respect, or worship dharma preachers. Wherever this dharma discourse goes, son of good family, it will play the role of the tathagata."

51 Then the entire congregation shouted its approval, "Excellent, excellent, blessed lord! We too will honor, revere, and respect the dharma preacher, who makes the dharma heard, in a manner befitting a tathagata. We will provide him with whatever he needs for complete happiness. We will disseminate this dharma discourse widely and protect it. And thus, this dharma discourse will persevere for a long time."

52 Then at that time, the blessed lord considered the congregation in its entirety and replied, "Excellent, excellent! Hey truly, sons of good family, you should do just that! When you listen to this dharma discourse remain indifferent to physical and mental discomfort, even if you suffer assaults, humiliations, verbal abuses, threats, or curses. Copy this dharma discourse and inspire others to copy it. Provide the dharma preacher, who makes the dharma heard, with whatever he needs for complete happiness. For such a person is a kingdom; he is an island; he is a city to be guarded from fears, catastrophes, troubles, and irritations. Constantly concentrate your attentions upon that son or daughter of good family."

Verses

Then at that time, the blessed lord spoke these verses:

Listen, sons of good family, without distraction,
lest in the last time you suffer.

One encounters the birth of a buddha only occasionally
over the course of hundreds of thousands of millions of aeons.
So, those who hear of the buddha's qualities and conceive strong faith
in them will attain samadhi without difficulty.

Suppose that someone makes offerings to the buddhas—
money and grain, garments and ornaments,
perfumes and garlands and balms—
for millions of aeons, like the sands of the Ganges River.

Now suppose someone else conceives strong faith in this sutra,
and then listens to it, recites it, and has it copied—
there is no measure for the latter person's merit,
so great is its magnitude as taught by the tathagata.

Suppose someone were to constantly serve a monastery zealously;
or were to always practice meditation while undistracted;
or were to give away his precious sons and daughters as a gift;
or were to sacrifice his hands and feet.

Yet, if someone else were to preserve this sutra,
he would obtain more merit.

This excellent sutra is a source of wealth,
and through it all bad rebirths are averted forever.
It is a source of money and grain as well.

Moreover, someone who preserves this holy sutra
will have no difficulty acquiring every good quality;
nor will he have difficulty obtaining longevity, strength, and vigor.

He will behold **Amitabha** Buddha, the leader.
I have prophesied that he will awaken as a buddha.
Never again will he experience evil.
He will see the Land of Bliss.

From now on, whatever karma he accumulates
will all be exhausted through anxiety,

or a sharp pain of the body, or even a headache.
But, it will never become calamitous for him.

In this very life, moreover, he will acquire good qualities,
all just as he has imagined and desired.

Always, therefore, monks and nuns,
laymen, laywomen, and kings, always,
should preserve this sutra, always,
and should show honor to its preserver always.

With perfume, and with garlands, and with balms,
they should pay it honor and have it copied,
after they conceive solemn respect for the dharma preacher
as if he were the tathagata, the blessed lord of men.

Otherwise in the last time they will be stricken by old age
        and disease,
and tormented by many thousands of tribulations.
They will be born wandering among the hells and as animals,
as abhorrent hermaphrodites and eunuchs,
congenitally blind, smelling putrid like corpses,
in second-rate families, and as women.

Always, the jealous, evildoers,
those conquered by hatred, and the avaricious,
having offered no reverence to the buddhas and dharma,
will be reborn in states such as these.
And once born there, they will experience misery.

Therefore, those who would preserve and proclaim this sutra
should also always worship it,
lest in the last time they suffer.

Those who would revile proponents of this sutra,
slandering, beating, and binding them,
are in fact reviling me.

One truly honors me by honoring this sutra's preserver.
Therefore, the dharma preachers—those who would
preserve, copy, and recite this sutra always—
are eternally worthy of honor,
and sweet, affectionate words should be spoken of them.

Avalokiteshvara's Discourse

53 Then, the bodhisattva noble Avalokiteshvara prostrated at the blessed lord's feet and said, "Blessed lord, I recollect an incantation named *the miracle of close examination*, which I heard and learned long ago in the presence of tathagata Jnanaketuprabhakara. Living beings who hear, learn, remember, recite, honor, copy, and incite others to copy this incantation attain the stage on the bodhisattva path at which they never stop progressing toward buddhahood. They acquire all the good qualities described by the tathagata. They satisfy all desires. They overcome every obstacle to spiritual progress. They attain samadhis. They become free of disease. They receive visions of buddhas and visions of bodhisattvas."

54 Then the blessed lord offered his approval, "Excellent, excellent, son of good family! Turn the wheel of dharma! The tathagata authorizes it."

55 Then the bodhisattva noble Avalokiteshvara paid homage to all tathagatas in the ten directions and recited this mantra:

56 *Homage to all tathagatas, the fulfillers of all hopes! Homage to noble Avalokiteshvara, the bodhisattva, the highly compassionate! Here is the mantra: HA HA HA HA For me! Preserve! Preserve! Serene! Very serene! Destroyer of every evil! Look down, compassionate one! Focus on your aspi-*

ration for awakening! Look everywhere! Remember me! Remember the vow
you made in the past! Through that vow, fulfill all my wishes! Purify a bud-
dhafield! May no harm come to me! By the power of the buddha! SVAHA

Here is the mantra: Blazing! Blazing! Brightly blazing! Remove my mis-
deeds of body, my misdeeds of speech, my misdeeds of mind! Remove my
poverty! Look out! Look across! I long for a vision of the tathagatas and a
vision of the bodhisattvas. DHU DHU PA Show! Show yourself to me! May
all my merit grow! Homage to all tathagatas! Homage to Avalokiteshvara!
Remember your promise, great one! May this mantra succeed! SVAHA

57   While the incantation was being recited, the earth quaked. Great
     shouts of joy resounded. Heavenly flowers showered down.
     And the congregation cried its approval, "Excellent, excellent!
     Well said! Great being, your mantra, intended to protect be-
     ings, will also fulfill their every hope, guard them from horrors,
     remove their karma, and quiet anxious nightmares about their
     own deaths. We, all of us, will likewise preserve and honor this
     mantra."

58   Avalokiteshvara said, "Suppose a son of good family has a deep
     desire for something excellent, like hearing the tathagata predict
     that he will become a buddha; or seeing me face-to-face; or attain-
     ing samadhis; or visions of buddhas and bodhisattvas; or posses-
     sions and power; or rebirth in buddhafields.

59   "On the eighth day of the half month when the moon is waxing,
     he should purify himself, by washing his body and by adopting the
     eight upavasa vows. Then, in a sacred place empowered by the
     buddha, he should do puja with perfume and flowers, with flags
     and banners, and with full jars. Using flowers, garlands, and per-
     fumes, let him pay reverence to that sacred place, as well as to a
     dharma preacher, who is pure, well bathed, and dressed all in
     white. Then let that son of good family commit this dharma dis-
     course to writing. Sharing his roots of virtue with all beings; his
     heart filled with benevolence, sympathy, and compassion; fixing
     his mind upon the tathagata with profound reverence, he ought

to write the dharma discourse for as long as half a day, every day. From the eighth day of the half month, until the fifteenth day, he should perform this ritual every day.

60 "Just by writing the dharma discourse, a son of good family who follows these precise instructions will escape the consequences of his past evil deeds—even the five atrocities that have immediate consequences. Instead, he will abound in virtuous qualities, glow with vigor, and enjoy bodily comfort no matter what the circumstances. His passion, hatred, and delusion, as well as his conceit and anger, will fade away.

61 "The son of good family has already written down the dharma discourse. Now, he should position images of the tathagata and Avalokiteshvara facing east, near a **caitya** that contains a relic; both images must contain relics as well. In this place, let him perform the exalted rite for the tathagata with flowers, incense, perfumes, and lamps. From the eighth day until the fifteenth day of the half month, let him develop the thought of great compassion for all beings. At dawn, noon, and twilight daily, while eating only pure, white food; following the eight upavasa vows; having a friend to assist him; remaining free of conceit, hatred, and selfishness, he should perform the exalted rite and intone the incantation 108 times. Again at dawn, noon, and twilight, he should offer lamps, incense, and flowers to the image of Avalokiteshvara and then strike it with 108 jasmine blossoms. Let him burn incense to Vajrapani as well. Then after bowing deeply to the ten directions, he should throw a bali offering of flavorful milk-rice and **curd-rice** to the four directions: to the goddess Bhima in the west, Anopama in the east, and Shankhini in the north.

62 "After that, nothing will make him distraught, or anxious, or cause his mind to waver. Thus everybody is urged to perform the rite involving 108 recitations and 108 jasmine blossoms.

63 "A son of good family who has performed the preliminary rites according to these precise instructions should continue as follows on the fifteenth day of the fortnight, when the moon is full: Set up

four full jars. Make a gift of incense, sandalwood, frankincense, camphor, and four lamps. Decorate the ground with various fragrances, flags, painted cloths, banners, as well as gold and silver vessels. Cast a bali offering of yogurt, honey, milk-rice, and curd-rice—or other foods as available—to the four directions. After this is done, and after intoning the incantation over 108 jasmine blossoms, one by one, throw the flowers to the four directions as before. Lastly, intone the incantation over three sets of 108 jasmine blossoms, one by one, and strike the image of noble Avalokiteshvara with the blossoms.

64 "The image will then shake. There will be a loud roar and rays of light will shoot forth. The earth will quake. Afterwards, everything that son of good family does, whether done by choice or by obligation, will meet success. He will receive visions of tathagatas. He will ascend the stages of the bodhisattva path. Everybody will think him praiseworthy. His treasuries will overflow with wealth and his storerooms will overflow with grain. He will never be sick and will live a long time. Enemies, kings, princes, and government officials will all crave an audience with him. His servants will not have any afflictions, passions, anger, or delusion. Never again will he be separated from his loved ones. He will have great determination, fortitude, and strength. He will be resplendent. His senses will be sharp. He will be intelligent. He will feel sympathy for everybody. He will know dharma. Skipping to the end of the list: He will see the blessed lord buddha and noble Avalokiteshvara at the time of death, and will die suffused with love while reciting the dharma. He will be reborn just as he desires, wherever he sets his mind, whether in buddhafields or in the families of powerful universal emperors. And he will enjoy many thousand more benefits besides.

65 "Thus, blessed lord, this dharma discourse and incantation are sources of great virtue. Unless someone is empowered by the tathagata, he cannot hear this dharma discourse, or remember it, or worship it, or write it, or have it written, or place his faith in

it. Even if he comes into contact with this dharma discourse, he won't hear it. Or if he hears it, his mind will be distracted as he listens. He will not show it faith or honor.

66 "However, if someone does pay honor to this dharma discourse, his mind will be free of affliction and malice. If he copies it or has it copied, his mind will be unwavering. What is the reason? Just this: Because his previous evil actions have come to fruition, he must experience karma and be filled with doubt. But if he performs this ritual three times all his hopes will be fulfilled, even if he is guilty of the five atrocities that have immediate consequences. About this, let there be neither worry, nor disagreement, nor doubt."

67 Then the blessed lord offered his approval, "Excellent, excellent, son of good family! This dharma discourse will play the role of the tathagata for all beings."

Anopama's Discourse

68 After that, the great yakshini Anopama approached the blessed lord. She venerated him with many flowers and a double length of fine cloth. Then prostrating at his feet, Anopama said,

69 "Blessed lord, I clearly remember that, while you were staying at Ghoshila's park in Kaushambi, I took an oath to benefit all living beings. And so, since I know the inner secret of all sorcerers, lord, please permit me to share it, in order to benefit the many and comfort the many, as well as to fulfill every hope of monks and nuns, laymen and laywomen."

70 *Homage to all tathagatas! Here is the mantra: HA HA HI HI HU HU Run! Run! Nimbly! Nimbly! Quickly! Quickly! Great wise woman! Lady honored by all sorcerers! Laugh! Why do you stand? Limbs ornamented with gold and many-colored gems! PATA PATA BHARA BHARA BHIRI BHIRI BHURU BHURU Make all my endeavors succeed! Make my endeavors succeed! Give me—nam-tse hammarapati shulkshina—success! HA HA Lotus! Lotus! Great lotus! Brilliant! Brilliant! Greatly brilliant! Presence! Pres-*

ence! Manifest your presence! Here I am, fearsome lady! Here I am, fearsome lady! Work your magic for me! Give me success! Fulfill all my hopes! By the power of the buddhas! SVAHA

71 "Blessed lord, suppose someone wants something excellent, like wealth and grain, or to wield control over all living beings, or great power, or to be a king, or to be a sorcerer. Or maybe he wants to meet me face-to-face.

72 "On the eighth day of the half month when the moon is waxing, he should hire a painter, who has purified himself by adopting the eight upavasa vows, to paint the following scene on a new piece of cotton. (The cotton's fringes should be uncut and loose threads should be removed. The colors should not be mixed; the paints stored in new pots.) In the center, let him paint an image of the tathagata teaching the dharma. On the right, the noble **Vajrakrodha** brandishing a vajra, adorned with many ornaments, wearing flower garlands and strings of half-moon pearls, clothed all in white. On the left side, Anopama, golden like a stalk of sugarcane, adorned with many ornaments, clothed all in white, holding a lotus, and in the gesture of comforting.

73 "On the eighth day of the half month, the preliminary service should be performed in a holy place dedicated to the tathagata, containing a relic, by a sorcerer who has purified himself by adopting the eight upavasa vows, eating a porridge of milk and barley, and dressing all in white. After that, he should perform a puja with various flowers, fragrances, incense, and lamps. Following three such pujas, he should then recite the incantation in three sets of 108 recitations each. And after he recites the incantation over 108 jasmine blossoms, one by one, he should strike that image with the blossoms, repeating this procedure three times. Let him devote the very first flowers, incense, and fragrances to the tathagata and Vajrapani. As a bali offering, he should cast milk-rice and curd-rice—full of spices and alcohol—to the four directions. Finally, on the fifteenth day of the half month, when

the moon is full, he should make a bali offering and offer other available items, such as camphor, frankincense, sandalwood, and fenugreek, adhering to these exact rules. He should also offer two lamps burning fragrant oil.

74 "Then I will present myself right then and there in my own body and give him whatever reward he chooses: the attainment of samadhis, ability to fly, invisibility, kingship, status as a powerful universal emperor, status as a sorcerer, ability to find treasures, alchemical mastery, mind reading, longevity.

75 "Let him cultivate the thought of love for all living beings. Let him not be conceited, hateful, jealous, or selfish. Let him refuse to steal wealth belonging to **stupas**, to the dharma, or to the sangha. Let him have unwavering faith in the tathagatas.

76 "Blessed lord, if somebody performs this rite three times—even somebody guilty of the five atrocities that have immediate consequences—and if I do not respond, then may I not awaken to unsurpassed, complete, and perfect awakening. But I will not show myself to, nor will I enrich, anyone who lacks faith in the buddha; or to an unbeliever; or to someone whose actions are evil and unworthy but who will not change his ways because his mind is clouded by affliction and woe."

77 Then the blessed lord offered his approval, "Excellent, excellent, lady! Once again, lady, excellent! In your effort to help everybody, you have taught this particular mantra to errant creatures. Your sworn oath is the distinctive manifestation of great compassion that will enable you to establish all living beings in unsurpassed, complete, and perfect awakening. You should act just so."

Shankhini's Discourse

78 Then the great goddess Shankhini venerated the blessed lord with an abundance of flowers and fragrances. She circumambulated him, prostrated at his feet, and said,

79 "With the tathagata's authorization, I too will swear an oath. To guarantee that the tathagata's teachings endure, and to fulfill all hopes of those who preach dharma and study dharma, I offer a protective mantra. Blessed lord, please permit me this!"

80 *Homage! Homage to all tathagatas! OM Shankhini! Goddess! Come! Stay! Treasure! Winner of treasure! Make- make- maker of wealth! Make- make- maker of strength! Many different kinds of dresses and clothing! Pre- pre- server of life! Pro- pro- protector of life! Remember the tathagata! Remember your aspiration for awakening! Don't delay! Give me a gift! Shankhini! SVAHA*

81 "Someone who puts this mantra on his body will become more famous, more fabulous, more wealthy, more powerful, longer lived, and will exercise greater control over his enemies.

82 "Recite the mantra 108 times and make a bali offering to the four directions using whatever is available. Then perform the exalted rite for the tathagata with incense and frankincense. Offer a lamp. For twenty-one days cultivate the state of loving-kindness and maintain self-control. After that, I will fulfill every desire, except those that violate the true dharma. Perform this rite in a holy place or at the shrine of a god."

83 Then the blessed lord and congregation offered their approval, "Excellent, excellent, lady! Well said! Your oath has many virtues. In the future you too should act in just this way."

Bhima's Discourse

84 After that, the great goddess Bhima venerated the blessed lord with golden flowers, prostrated at his feet, and said,

85 "I too shall offer a mantra that grants all wishes, including those for gold, jewels, pearls, possessions, power, kingship, longevity, and control over one's enemies. I offer this mantra in order to benefit dharma-preachers, who make the dharma heard, as well

as those who write the dharma, as well as those who preserve, recite, and worship the dharma.

86 "Suppose there is a king or queen, monk or nun, layman or laywoman who preserves, honors, copies, or has someone else copy this dharma discourse. And suppose that he or she, filled with profound reverence for the tathagata, performs its rites as taught. Blessed lord, I will protect that person and guard him. I will grant him whatever reward he desires. I will guarantee that he has totally enough possessions and power. I will ensure his victory in disputes, wars, riots, and skirmishes. I will make his life prosper. I will protect his country and city. Blessed lord, please permit me this!"

87 *Homage to all tathagatas! Homage to all bodhisattvas, beginning with noble Avalokiteshvara and Vajrapani! OM Great goddess! Bhima! Fearsome lady! Victorious lady! Grantor of victory! Swift with glory! Swift with radiance! Receiver of a prophecy to buddhahood! Watching out for all living beings! Filled with the radiance of compassion! Obey the tathagata's command! Remember your promise. By the power of the buddhas: Give me a gift! Make me successful! Goddess! Great goddess! Goddess who speaks the truth! Bhima! Lady who can be trusted to tell the truth! Dweller in mystery! SVAHA*

88 "I spoke this mantra, empowered by the tathagata and authorized by the tathagata, with the intention of helping beings. Let a supplicant focus his mind on the precise object of his desire and recite this mantra. Then let him perform a puja in front of the tathagata with flowers, incense, fragrance, and lamps. Then let him cast a flavorful bali offering of milk-rice to the four directions. When the mantra is recited 108 times, I will satisfy his exact desire and fulfill all his hopes.

89 "Suppose someone really wants to see me in my true form. On the eighth day of the half month, he should hire a painter, who has taken the eight upavasa vows, to paint the following scene on a piece of cotton. (The cotton's fringes should be uncut and

loose threads should be removed. The colors should not be mixed; the paints stored in new pots.) In the middle, he should paint an image of the tathagata teaching the dharma. On the right, noble Avalokiteshvara giving a discourse. On the left, the great goddess Bhima, golden like a stalk of sugarcane, adorned with all ornaments, dressed in white, holding a pitcher of water and vial of medicine, in the gesture of comforting.

90 "Later on the eighth day, near a caitya that contains a relic, he should perform the preliminary service with flowers, incense, perfume, garlands, and balms. Let him then cast a bali offering of milk-rice and curd-rice to the four directions. Subsequently, on the fifteenth day of the half month, when the moon is full, a pure sorcerer should perform the exalted rite using flowers, incense, perfume, and lamps. Let him also make a flavorful bali offering, as well as an offering of white foods, depending upon what is available. Then let him fill his mind with love and compassion for every living being and strike the image with 108 jasmine blossoms, after reciting the mantra over each blossom individually.

91 "Right then and there, I will present myself in my own body. I will give him whatever he wants as a reward: kingship and power, the ability to fly, the ability to find treasures, alchemical mastery, or status as a sorcerer. And I will do whatever else he wants done: I will ward off untimely death, cure all disease, crush enemy armies, provide sons, give him riches, or make everybody love him.

92 "Blessed lord, if I do not fulfill all hopes—even if a supplicant is guilty of the five atrocities that have immediate consequences— then may I not awaken to unsurpassed, complete, and perfect awakening . . . except, that is, if the supplicant condemns the true dharma or is skeptical about the three jewels."

93 The blessed lord affirmed, "Excellent, excellent, lady! Once again, excellent! Lady, you have sworn an oath for the good and happiness of all beings. You have sworn to guarantee that this dharma discourse long endures. Therefore, lady, always make sure that you always heed your oath."

94 Then, at that time, the earth quaked and a rain of divine blossoms came pouring down. The whole congregation offered its approval, "Excellent, excellent! Well said! This oath will fulfill the hopes of all beings."

Reprising the Merit of the Sutra

95 Once again noble Avalokiteshvara, the bodhisattva mahasattva, addressed the blessed lord, "How much merit will sons or daughters of good family accumulate when they copy, recite, have others copy, disseminate, read, study, and worship this dharma discourse?"

96 The blessed lord replied, "Instead, Avalokiteshvara, I shall test you. Explain as best you can!"

97 Avalokiteshvara responded, "Actually, blessed lord, you should explain this. For the tathagata, nothing is unseen, unheard, or unknown."

98 The blessed lord then said, "Son of good family, even by means of analogy one cannot describe how much merit people will make if they copy, have others copy, recite, worship, disseminate, read, or study this dharma discourse. Why? Even after someone gives a gift that satisfies the personal desires of all living beings, they are still not liberated from old age, disease, death, sadness, lamentation, misery, ill will, or anxiety. Though they might delight in sensual pleasures for hundreds of thousands of years, because they are not liberated they will still experience torments in the hells, the animal realm, the world of Yama, or that of the hungry ghosts. But after living beings hear this dharma discourse, after they worship it and disseminate it, after they consider its meaning and practice its practices, they definitely do become liberated from old age, disease, death, sadness, lamentation, misery, ill will, and anxiety, as well as from all hells, births as animals, and Yama's realm. This is why the tathagata does not reckon that quantity of merit, even by means of analogy.

99 "Suppose that, in honor of this dharma discourse, a son of good family gives away a single golden flower the size of a mustard seed, or a single fruit, or a single flag, or a musical instrument, or perfume, or cloth, or a seat, or an ornament. Suppose that he copies this dharma discourse, or has another copy it, or preserves it, or recites it, or worships it, or proclaims it at length to others, or praises and worships someone who preaches its dharma.

100 "Now suppose that, while the tathagata is still alive, another son of good family worships and reveres the tathagata and his retinue by performing a puja in their presence. Moreover, for hundreds of thousands of years this second son of good family furnishes the tathagata with whatever he needs for total happiness, such as perfume, garlands, balms, banners, and flags. Moreover, he constructs monasteries, promenades, and parks. Moreover, he builds a three-and-one-half-mile-high stupa entirely out of precious metals and gemstones; or one hundred such stupas, or one thousand. And suppose that he performs a puja in honor of the tathagata with sublime rites that last for hundreds of thousands of years.

101 "Because the first son of good family copies, has others copy, preserves, reads, worships, and disseminates this dharma discourse, he will accumulate more merit than the second. A puja performed in the tathagata's presence does not produce greater merit; nor surely does giving gifts that allow beings to delight in sensual pleasures.

102 "Therefore, that being the case, sons and daughters of good family, kings and princes, royal ministers and royal advisers should always worship this dharma discourse. They should conceive of spiritual benefactors who proclaim, discuss, and summarize the meaning of this dharma discourse as if they were the tathagata himself. And after they worship those spiritual benefactors, they should listen to this dharma discourse, accept it, remember it, recite it, and keep it in their thoughts.

103 "Indeed, they should think, 'Our attainments are well attained. The dharma discourse we have heard reveals the path of those

who take the wrong path, of those who mistakenly perceive worth in the worthless, of those who mistakenly perceive permanence in the impermanent, of those who mistakenly find satisfaction in the unsatisfactory. For us, this dharma discourse has played the role of the tathagata, for its purpose is to liberate us fully from rebirth in the hells, or among the animals, or in Yama's realm.'"

104 Avalokiteshvara said, "This dharma discourse is proclaimed to all beings for a great purpose: to act as a tathagata."

105 The blessed lord said, "Son of good family, in the last time, in the last period, this dharma discourse will proceed to the south. The monks, nuns, laymen, laywomen, kings, princes, ministers, and royal advisers in that region will become vessels for the dharma—worshiping, preserving, and reciting this dharma discourse. They will place their faith in it and will trust it. If this dharma discourse travels to the north, east, or west, however, the people there will be engrossed in other activities. They will not listen to this dharma discourse, nor will they place their faith in it, trust it, or worship it. Lazy and bored, they will be too distracted, thinking about their families, slaves, possessions, power, laughing, festivals, performances, dancing, singing, jealousies, and petty slights. They will not listen to, trust, or worship this dharma discourse. And thus they will not be liberated from old age, disease, death, sadness, lamentation, misery, ill will, and anxiety; or from rebirth among the hungry ghosts or Yama's realm.

106 "Therefore, that being the case, sons and daughters of good family who wish to extricate themselves from all **miserable rebirths** should pay homage to this dharma discourse. They should worship and preserve it, honor it, proclaim it to others, and memorize it. In the event of fights, riots, nightmares, and evil omens; to avoid an untimely death due to cows, wild animals, or monsters; to avert all sicknesses, fears, and disasters: they should worship and recite this dharma discourse. Or, after raising it on a banner, they should worship it and carry it forth in procession with abundant perfume, flowers, incense, and musical instruments. Every

possible plague and catastrophe will be averted if, after they cast a bali offering to the four directions, they pay homage to this dharma discourse with flowers, incense, and perfume."

Verses, Second Set

Then, at that time, the blessed lord spoke these verses:

Accept this samadhi, Ananda,
spoken by buddhas in previous lives!

Suppose someone were to fill the **three realms** with jewels
of many kinds, and then offer them as a gift
to the buddhas and dharma, continually, without distraction.
Yet, if someone else were to preserve this sutra,
his merit would be greater than that.

Suppose someone who has placed his faith fully in the buddha
were to commission the building of monasteries and shrines.
However, were he to offer profound reverence to this sutra,
the material offering would not be at all comparable to the worship.

Suppose someone were to give away a single flower—
or, likewise, a garment or garland or balm.
Now, suppose someone else were to give
the gift of a gold coin for worshiping this sutra,
after he conceives a benevolent aspiration for awakening.
The latter would obtain more merit than the former.

If a bodhisattva disseminates this samadhi
and teaches it to living beings,
and thereby proceeds toward unsurpassed awakening:
no merit is at all comparable to his.

Thus truly you should preserve this sutra,
as well as copy, recite, and disseminate it,
for you have heard its benefits,
and cultivated love for all beings accordingly.

Lest in the last time you may suffer:
reborn in the hells or among the hungry ghosts.

Oppressed by the torments of old age, disease, and death;
mind petrified with fear at the moment of death;
heaving deep sighs again and again;
naively searching from face to face,
wondering, "Who will protect me? Who will be my refuge?"
because you have not performed puja to the tathagata.

Stealing property belonging to buddha, dharma, and sangha
must lead to Yama's dreadful realm.
Such a thief will never find any refuge:
no children, no wife, no friends, no family,
no kingdom, no laughter, no dancing,
no wealth, no grain, no clothing, no ornaments.

Having lost everything again and again,
that fool will experience misery and suffering, as well as horror.
What person of simple understanding would not have faith,
after he has heard about that misery and these benefits?

Constantly, therefore, monks and nuns
laymen, laywomen, and kings, always,
should preserve this sutra, forever,
and should perpetually pay homage to its preserver.

The Concluding Discourse

107 Then venerable Ananda spoke, "Blessed lord, I accept this dharma discourse. Regarding this dharma discourse as my teacher, I will preserve it, worship it, and make it known it to all beings."

108 The blessed lord replied, "Ananda, suppose you fail to preserve, recite, worship, or disseminate the totality of my dharma teachings which you have heard and remembered. In that case, you would not offend me and would not have disobeyed me. I would still consider you my disciple. Now suppose you fail to preserve, recite, worship, disseminate, or remember this dharma discourse. In that case, you would offend me and have disobeyed me. You would no longer be my disciple. Therefore Ananda, that being the case, honor this dharma discourse and preserve it. As the tathagata's unsurpassed, complete, and perfect awakening, this dharma discourse will play the role of the tathagata for all beings in the last time, in the last period."

109 Indeed, while the blessed lord was preaching this dharma discourse, sixty thousand beings stopped clinging to existence, their minds completely freed of the sources from which karma streams forth. Seven hundred attained the samadhis of bodhisattvas. Five hundred received predictions that they would be reborn in various buddhafields. Ninety thousand became completely free of all mental filth. They eliminated all possibility of being reborn in **situations unfavorable for practicing dharma**, miserable rebirths, or other evil destinies.

110 Then noble Avalokiteshvara, the bodhisattva mahasattva, spoke yet again, "Blessed lord, in the last time, in the last period, this dharma discourse will play the role of the tathagata for sons of good family who hear it, preserve it, esteem it, worship it, and copy it. They are destined to be reborn in whichever buddhafields they choose.

111 "But in the last time, in the last period, there will also be people who find diverse motley distractions in laughter, performances,

singing, and music. They will be blinded by passion, anger, and delusion. They will mistakenly perceive sex as a sport. They will mistakenly perceive permanence in the impermanent. They will be in thrall to jealousy, selfishness, and immorality. Such people will not worship this dharma discourse, or esteem it, or place faith in it, or trust it, or preserve it, or listen to it, or practice its practices. And thus, after they completely squander the sweet fruits of earlier good deeds, they will undergo the suffering of the hells, where misery and despair are manifold. And then after they experience suffering for many hundreds of millions of aeons, they will again be reborn in the hells, or as animals, or in Yama's realm.

112 "Yet, although they have been under the influence of harmful friends for a very long time, they will turn away from those bad influences for just an instant, after which they will feel penitent. That being the case, therefore, restrain body, speech, and mind. Have unwavering faith in the buddha, dharma, and sangha. Think thoughts of universal love. Be rid of jealous, selfish, and immoral thoughts. Be rid of anger."

113 Then the entire congregation worshiped the blessed lord—each according to his own accumulated merit—with celestial flowers, fragrances, garlands, balms, clothes, and ornaments. With voices shouting cries of joy, and with heavenly tambourines, cymbals, and song, they offered up their praise: "Excellent, excellent, blessed lord! Well said! This great dharma discourse will guarantee that the tathagata's teachings persevere for the benefit of all beings."

114 Then venerable Ananda asked the blessed lord, "What is this dharma discourse named? How shall we remember it?"

115 The blessed lord replied, "Ananda, preserve this dharma discourse with the name 'Ascending the Stages of the Bodhisattva Path as Authorized by All Tathagatas.' Preserve it with the name 'The Gathering of Great Beings Who Work Marvels Through Psychic Powers.' Preserve it with the name 'The Splendid Vision in

Which One Observes Living Beings and Displays Buddhafields Through the Empowerment of All Tathagatas.'"

Conclusion

116 The blessed lord said this. Enraptured, all the bodhisattva maha-sattvas led by noble Avalokiteshvara, Manjushri, and Vajrapani, all the great disciples, all the Shakras, Brahmas, and world protectors, the four great kings, all the great yakshinis led by Anopama, Vimalaprabha, Dyutidhari, Bhima, Shri, Shankhini, and Hariti, all the gods, nagas, yakshas, gandharvas, **asuras**, **garudas**, **kinnaras**, and **mahoragas**, and that entire well-organized congregation of monks, nuns, laymen, and laywomen rejoiced at the blessed lord's words.

INTERPRETIVE ESSAY

Reading Sutras in Theory and in Practice

THE COOL FACTOR

Every two years I teach The Buddhist Imaginary, a class introducing students to the doctrinal and institutional histories of Buddhism in India. The syllabus is not particularly innovative. Modeled on a course I myself took as an undergraduate, it begins by setting Shakyamuni in his historical context. The class then recounts the buddha's life story, explicates the four noble truths, follows the rise of the Mahayana, and concludes with Tantra. In the end, the final exam accomplishes that which Brahmin rivals and Muslim warriors did not: the end of Buddhism in India.

At least for most students that is the end. But recently one came away marked for life. Late in the semester I had students read *The Splendid Vision in Which One Observes Living Beings and Reveals Buddhafields Through the Empowerment of All Tathagatas*, after which we discussed the sutra's characters, rituals, and ideals, much as I do later in this essay. Following the discussion, a student came up and asked me how to spell *bodhisattva* in Devanagari script. I showed her and did not think about it again until the final exam, when she uncovered her new tattoo—बोधिसत्त्व—inspired by the *Splendid Vision*. Frankly, I was not altogether pleased that the student had marked herself so. The last thing I wanted was to hear parents' complaints. Still, since this was neither her first tattoo nor, probably, her last, I was also not altogether displeased that the student had inked herself as a bodhisattva. At least I knew that she had done the reading.

Are you now wondering whether, when reading the sutra, you missed an injunction to ink बोधिसत्त्व on your left shoulder in greenish black? Not exactly. In a short speech given by the great goddess Shankhini, the *Splendid Vision* promises that people who place her mantra on their bodies will be amply rewarded. Shankhini describes such varied blessings as treasure, strength, protection, and different kinds of dresses and clothing, not to mention being fabulous (§81). For some, the satisfaction of any of these desires might be a fine reason to tattoo themselves. However, when I asked my student why she had done it, her explanation was, simply, "It's cool."

At the time I was frustrated by this blank answer. By calling the tattoo cool, the student obviously was pointing to some kind of special allure or charm. But what? Did she seek a daily reminder of a vow to become a buddha in order to release all beings from suffering? Did she hope, per Shankhini's promise, that by inking this word into her skin she would become rich, famous, and powerful? Or maybe she did not feel like talking, since class was over, the test was over, and she was just eager to get away for the summer. Certainly, I had no right to demand a fuller answer, however frustrated my curiosity.

In retrospect, it is just as well that I did not interrogate her further. Now there is a moral to the story. The student's reaction to the *Splendid Vision* suggests that this is a powerful text; its sweeping claims remain compelling to this day. Yet, while one might observe a cause and effect relationship between the sutra and the tattoo, the nature of that connection remains obscure. Who can say how or why the *Splendid Vision* moved her so, except to say that it entailed a "cool factor." She inked herself बोधिसत्त्व because it was a cool thing to do.

As indefinable values go, cool merits a spot somewhere between beauty and truth. Enchanting yet impenetrable, cool is the mystery that sits there right on the surface. Cool moves us, inspires us to act, though we cannot quite discern whence its power derives. Aristotle envisioned the heavens as a perfect sphere. At the center point, he described an entity so supernal in its attraction, and so stable in itself, that it was able to cause all motion, even though it remained perfectly still.[1] This unmoved mover is the very epitome of cool: beautiful, desired, complete in itself, unattainable, unperturbed, emotionally moving. Indeed, Shakyamuni is not unlike Aristotle's perfect entity. In the *Splendid Vision*, the buddha sits on a throne, unmoving, while he sheds a light of universal love that touches all creatures great and small. This light, in turn, moves beings to forsake their daily pleasures in pursuit of the unparalleled perfection at the heart of the radiance (§10). If the buddha is cool, then maybe my tattooed student really was a bodhisattva.

Forget the student. Forget the buddha. Consider Shulkshina and Shulivujna, the man and woman discussed in this book's introduction, whose names were inserted into the *Splendid Vision*'s mantras. The sixth-century manuscript was created for their benefit: to free Shulkshina and Shulivujna from suffering and bring them blessings. Frankly, we don't know whether Shulkshina and Shulivujna themselves were responsible for this gesture or whether it was done on their behalf; whether they appreciated it or whether it was a secret gift. But even if we did know such facts—indeed, even if we read every book that Shulkshina and Shulivujna had read, heard every discourse they heard, visited every place they lived, and met every person they loved—we would still not know everything these two individuals thought of the *Splendid Vision*.

Shulkshina and Shulivujna are cool: not in the James Dean sense, but in the sense of being desirable yet unreachable; evidently significant yet ultimately mysterious. As a curious and intelligent reader of the *Splendid Vision* don't you want to learn more about Shulkshina and Shulivujna—especially what they thought of the sutra's astounding claims and complex rites? Doesn't the fact that we have these names in the Sanskrit manuscript transform this rather ordinary Mahayana sutra into something extraordinary, bringing it to life? This isn't just some book out of a library. It touched people's hands, brains, and hearts, in unknowable but movingly imaginable ways. Hearing the names, don't you feel your other senses enlivened? There you are in the courtyard of their fine Himalayan home, strewn with rugs and cushions, wisps of exotic sandalwood smoke rise and spread as Shulkshina and Shulivujna intone solemnities in praise of the three jewels.

It is difficult to take something called the cool factor seriously. Yet, we must. For despite the cheesy name, this factor points to a systemic flaw in our commonsense approach to reading religious literature. The remainder of this subsection considers that flaw, while the following two subsections suggest an alternative mode of approach before we turn midway through this essay to the *Splendid Vision*—from theory to practice.

Are you surprised that this essay, which promises an interpretation of the *Splendid Vision*, does not directly discuss the sutra's contents until its midpoint? After all, essays of this sort usually focus on situating sutras in their original contexts. They presume that the reader has little familiarity with the social milieu in which a sutra was written, or the intellectual puzzles it was meant to solve, and they provide the missing data. Were this such an essay, it might have, from the start, expressed wonder at how Shulkshina and Shulivujna understood the *Splendid Vision*; what the sutra meant to them; how it affected them religiously. But because inquiries into religious value and meaning are so abstract, it would have then grounded its answers concretely, by discussing the specific doctrines that most likely would have moved Shulkshina and Shulivujna to preach the sutra, or listen to a preacher, or write it down during the prescribed rituals. In this way, a more typical interpretive essay may have presupposed a chain of reasoning whereby intention explains meaning explains value, with intentions being framed in terms of distinctly Buddhist doctrines.

This seems so indisputably normal. But do you notice a sleight of hand? This reimagined essay began with a question about Shulkshina and Shulivujna. Frustrated by the unknowability of human beings' inner experience, however, it shifted attention to a matter that is possible to discuss openly—doctrine. Religious doctrines can be systematized, analyzed for logical consistency, and situated in complex webs of intertextuality. For this reason, our usual approach to ancient Indian Buddhism treats doctrines as the primary facts, and treats Buddhists as if they are agents of those facts. Ideas are put before human beings, even though human beings must logically come first. The cool factor calls attention to this stealthy inversion. Coolness is simply shorthand for the recognition that, since human behavior is complex, inflected by circumstance, often inchoate, and sometimes deceptive, we cannot approach the *Splendid Vision* assuming a linear cause and effect relationship between the sutra's words and the inner or outer religiosity of its readers, any more than we can fully know why my student tattooed herself बोधिसत्त्व after reading the *Splendid Vision*. Hypotheses aside, a humanistically sensitive reading of the *Splendid Vision* will begin with an acknowledgment of our own ignorance. This sutra, like the human heart, is a rag and bone shop, crammed with undiscovered junk—some timeworn, some foul, some contemporary, some cool.

This acknowledgment demands that we reconsider the types of information we seek from the sutra: How do we read it? How do we use it? What is it good for? Of course we might appreciate its chromatic highlights as we would curiosities in a Baroque still life. Instead of gutted guinea fowls or the graceful arch of a French tulip, however, we are treated to an array of medieval Buddhist arcana: proto-Tantric ritual, the Mahayana cult of the book, visions of the end times, and so on. But the cool factor alerts us: this approach can bring us only so far, and not necessarily where we want to go.

To clarify this last point, let us consider sociologist Robert Segal's now classic essay "In Defense of Reductionism."[2] Segal argued that secular scholars deceive themselves insofar as they operate on the presupposition that insider categories and insider explanations are sufficient bases for comprehending religious behaviors. Segal's examples focus on the belief in god. He proposes that any secular scholar who claims to fully represent, or fully empathize with, believers' own religious beliefs must be mistaken. Segal's logic is simple. Believers are, first and foremost, people who believe in god's actual existence. In their guts they know that god is real. A scholar who tries to explicate religion wholly from an insider's point of view, accordingly, would have to feel god in his viscera, like a believer. Can a scholar who experiences god as real, and who writes from that experience, also claim to be secular and agnostic? Segal says no. In this, he is not judging the quality of outsider versus insider research. He is clarifying presuppositions and perspectives. Within the secular academy, Segal holds, religion can never be explained solely on its own terms. Religious explanations of religion can never be primary.

Actually, Segal takes his argument a step further, proposing that "it is impossible for a nonbeliever to accept a believer's own interpretation of religion as even the believer's own true one."[3] In other words, secular academics must assume that religious believers (unintentionally) lie to themselves, and to others, in their beliefs. A nonbeliever must be skeptical about any and all insider claims to truth based in religious doctrine. On the same logic as before: to act otherwise would require the nonbeliever to entertain the possibility that the belief in god is legitimate, and thus not to be a true nonbeliever. To conclude this line of reasoning, Segal proposes that, for an outsider, everything religious insiders say about the objective dimensions of their own religiosity is incomplete, if not incorrect.[4]

Bringing this back to the *Splendid Vision*, we can understand Segal as saying: unless you and I are devout Buddhists, an interpretive essay that discusses the sutra only in terms of its insider, buddhological value must be incomplete, at best. Such an essay may even be considered deceitful if it were to claim that insider terms and insider concerns are the only terms and concerns that matter. Of course, I will not do that.

On the face of it, Segal sounds rather strident. Whenever I teach his essay, my students dislike it, even if they agree with it, because it seems so uncompromising. But despite the cold logic, Segal is talking about the cool factor. He is saying that religious believers are no different from any other human beings in that they "have no automatic, privileged, incorrigible entrée to the true nature of their behavior."[5] And as an observer of human behavior, Segal is not alone in this cool view. Recent advances in experimental psychology and neurophysiology have begun to demonstrate in unambiguous ways that it is materially impossible for human beings to know themselves fully, or be lamps unto themselves fully; to know exactly why they do what they do, or be able to articulate the motivations for their actions explicitly, in verbal maxims that can then be systematized in doctrinal treatises. Experiments on cognitive dissonance, for instance, have demonstrated the degree to which our personal preferences and desires are shaped, not by our independent free wills, but by a preconscious need for a sense of self-consistency.[6] Likewise, functional MRI brain-imaging techniques have yielded a picture of the brain as physically incapable of autonomy. Through social interactions, human beings literally change each other's brains—and minds—in ways that we can neither predict fully nor control.[7] Not only are we strangers to each other, but also, in the words of experimental psychologist Timothy Wilson, we are strangers to ourselves, for a great deal of our personality and identity is determined by what Wilson calls "mental processes that are inaccessible to consciousness but that influence judgments, feelings, or behavior."[8]

I return to this body of scientific scholarship later in the essay. For now I mention it, along with Robert Segal, to explain why this interpretive essay did not begin by focusing directly on the *Splendid Vision*'s ancient doctrines and community, though that may be what you expected. Any attempt to take the *Splendid Vision*'s statements about itself or its audience at face value is bad history because it is bad anthropology. Take this as a first principle in the study of religion: just because somebody is able to read ancient texts in their original language does not mean he is also able to read people. But in the end, people matter, not texts.

IN DEFENSE OF PRESENTISM

Although the *Splendid Vision* is a Buddhist text, there is more to it than that, and this essay is largely concerned with that "more." The *Splendid Vision* provides an opportunity for considering who we are as human beings, how religious texts address our humanity, and the implications of this dynamic for our reading practices. That said, however, we must now take a detour through Buddhist doctrine, for this approach to the *Splendid Vision* entails a critique of Buddhism's fundamental value: enlightenment.

We are strangers to ourselves. Let this statement sit a moment, as I recall for you some rudiments of Buddhist lore. Shakyamuni is the awakened buddha. Born to a life of innocent privilege, he was shocked to learn at the age of twenty-nine that human beings get sick, get old, and die. For six years, he sought a means of ultimate escape from this fate, finding his solution at the age of thirty-five. Shakyamuni analyzed himself and his world with an inerrant and critical eye; he saw reality pure and true; he was enlightened; he was free. For the next forty-five years, Shakyamuni taught others how to be enlightened like himself. Doctrinally speaking, Buddhism is the religion of enlightenment.

As an extension of this principle, Shakyamuni's followers have long characterized the buddha as *all-knowing*. The exact nature and scope of his enlightened omniscience is a matter of fierce sectarian controversy, but at the very least, the sects agree: Shakyamuni possessed perfect self-knowledge. For insiders, a buddha is definitively no stranger to himself. If a buddha's mind is obscured by even an iota of cognitive darkness then he is not a buddha. Indeed, beyond the buddha, according to the *Splendid Vision*, even the monks and nuns in the sutra's audience had perfect self-control over their intellects and emotions (§2). So, when an outsider field like experimental psychology proposes that human beings cannot avoid some degree of self-estrangement, it is also proposing that the insider ideal of perfect enlightenment is biologically untenable. From this perspective, Buddhism is founded on a fundamental misapprehension of our biological humanity.

Yet, enlightenment is not an exclusively Buddhist value; the problematization of enlightenment is not a quandary for Buddhism alone. In English, we find the term *enlightenment* used in (at least) three distinct realms of discourse. Buddhists use this word to characterize the cognitive state associated with buddhahood. Intellectual historians use it to name a school of rationalist philosophy that flourished in Europe during the seventeenth and eighteenth centuries. Protestant Christians use it to describe the grace of the holy spirit, whereby god himself touches the human heart. Although the three uses appear to be quite distinct, there is, in fact, a common denominator. Buddhists, philosophers, and Protestants all use enlightenment to indicate an ideal of human perfection. In the case of Shakyamuni, it is said that he was enlightened when, under the tree, he saw everything *just as it is*, and through this profound insight was liberated from suffering and rebirth. Thus, an enlightened buddha is held to be perfectly wise and perfectly free. In the case of European history, enlightenment philosophers proposed that it is possible for the human mind to understand the world in full and to act upon that understanding in completely appropriate and regular ways. In other words, human beings are capable of full rationality and this rationality is the basis of social and personal freedoms. In the case of Protestant Christianity, god's enlightenment opens a human being's heart to faith—so that she sees the world just as it is, as god's providential domain. Though the differences are vast, Buddhists, European philosophers, and Protestants all use enlightenment to designate an existential state that combines perfect insight with a promise of perfect freedom.

To take enlightenment seriously as a positive value entails an ideal of human perfectibility, no matter whether one is a Himalayan Buddhist, a philosophe in a powdered wig, or an austere Puritan. For a champion of enlightenment, people can understand themselves and their world in a thoroughgoing manner, though some will attribute that insight to meditation, while others will seek its source in scientific rationality, and still others in god's holy touch. Likewise, enlightenment's proponents expect that we can guide our lives and make choices that directly harmonize with this profound insight, rather than being buffeted by unconscious cognitive processes, emotional drives, or forces of circumstance.

We often use metaphors and images to clarify abstract concepts. In that spirit, let us envision these three forms of enlightenment as forming a braid: three strands interwoven, over and under, in and around, to create a single thick ideological rope. Each makes the others seem a little more comprehensible, perhaps even credible. Enlightenment as a value associated with the progress of modern science allows us to grasp, and thus maybe accept, the enlightenment Shakyamuni discovered while meditating under the bodhi tree, which in turn allows us to better understand and empathize with the inner enlightenment that the Protestant experiences as the light of grace. And of course, as with a braid, there is no primary strand. In following the braid from strand to strand, we may begin with any of the three. Given that every strand is as necessary as every other to maintaining the structural integrity of the whole, it is likewise true that if one strand frays, the other two will be affected. A braided rope is strong because it is woven, but the price of that strength is that unraveling one strand from the whole unravels them all.

So it is that the earlier discussion of the cool factor, which voiced misgivings as to the value scholars place on perfect understandability, opened up an intellectual space within which it was sensible to doubt the Buddhist view of omniscience as an entailment of enlightenment. This little untwisting of the braid, in turn, looses other questions, other problems. How are ideals of human enlightenment formed in relationship to texts? Do religious texts, in particular, function to instantiate and inculcate such ideals? What rhetorical strategies might authors of religious texts employ to represent their creations as enlightened? Or alternatively, what interpretive strategies might readers adopt in order to affirm their scriptures as enlightened? How might attention to the category "scripture"—a category of divine light that is deeply indebted to sixteenth-century Protestant Christian theology and hermeneutics—guide our reading of the *Splendid Vision*? This last question will be the focus of the next subsection.

This study of the *Splendid Vision* does not presuppose human perfectibility as an orienting ideal. Beginning with the obscurities of the cool factor, it happily accepts that indeterminacy, limitation, bias, and ignorance are constitutive dimensions of our common humanity. This is one reason why this essay does not endeavor to provide abundant data about the sutra in its original context; it offers some, but not nearly as much as it might. Rather than explicating the *Splendid Vision* as a source of truth—truth of dharma, truth of history—this essay treats the sutra as a creative work of literature. For me, the sutra's art lies in how its authors use the imaginary figure of an omniscient and enlightened buddha in order to convey their limited understanding and vision of the cosmos to other imperfect human beings. Enlightenment, in this study, is not a supreme realization but a bit of all-too-human rhetoric. Perfection lies, not in the sutra's ideals, but in its anonymous author's prosaic mobilization of those ideals. Indeed, even Shulkshina and Shulivujna, though they were flesh and blood once, are not so now. How could they be? Do you imagine that because we know their names we can really get into their heads and hearts? No, Shulkshina and Shulivujna here are characters in an academic fiction—names as readymades. They provide a ready-made point of departure for imagining the *Splendid Vision*'s audience and working through issues related to its reception as living scripture.

The principal question here is not, what does the sutra mean, but, rather, how does the sutra *work*? This is a modern question speaking to a modern sensibility. To address it I have elected to use a modern category—scripture—as a lens through which to elucidate the *Splendid Vision*—an ancient Indian Buddhist text. I do not focus on the category scripture because I want to assimilate Buddhism to Christianity, but rather because I want to highlight the hybridity of our reading practices. Read in the twenty-first century, the *Splendid Vision* is neither a purely ancient text nor a pristinely Buddhist text. There is something awkward about the anachronism of categorizing a Buddhist sutra as a scripture. By attending to this discomfort, we are forced to confront the dynamism of our reading practices. By paying attention to how we re-create the text when we read it, we open ourselves up to being marked by it in turn. Just think of my student's tattoo.

Technically speaking, *scripture* is used here as a heuristic category. That is to say, structures of thought associated with the interpretation of scripture provide a pattern or code that we can bring to bear on the *Splendid Vision*. You may be familiar with the story of Archimedes, the Greek mathematician who discovered a means for calculating the volume and density of irregularly shaped objects. While puzzling over how to determine whether a crown was made of solid gold or a gold-silver alloy, Archimedes sank down in his bath and then sprang right back up, for in seeing the displacement of water he also saw the solution to his puzzle. Legend holds that Archimedes ran naked through the streets shouting, *Eureka*, I found it! Indeed, the word *heuristic* derives from the same root as *eureka*. Like water for Archimedes who was seeking to calculate a volume of gold, a heuristic need not have a natural or necessary relationship to the phenomenon it is meant to clarify. Thus, our heuristic, scripture, has no exact cognate in Sanskrit or classic Buddhist doctrine. Yet, we might use this category heuristically to highlight and illuminate deep structures in the *Splendid Vision* that would otherwise remain invisible.

Historians sometimes disparage the use of heuristic categories, fretting that the imposition of modern concepts and perspectives onto nonmodern phenomena must result in anachronisms that distort true understandings of the past. Such historians hold that scholars ought to restrict themselves to using intellectual patterns or codes that would have been known to people living in the original time and context. For them, the only valid analytic categories are those that emerge directly from the data itself. Such historians condemn as *presentist* studies, like this essay, that would read the present into the past. It was to address such qualms that I introduced the cool factor in the previous section, and problematized enlightenment in this one. The critique of presentism begins with the assumption that, at least in the ideal, historians must try to understand and represent historical phenomena as they are, on their own terms alone, without personal bias affecting the representation. As I have already indicated, this position is debatable. We have no choice but to be presentist, at least to some degree. Our choice lies in how we bring the realities of our present lives to bear upon our interactions with the past.

In addition to *Eureka*, Archimedes is also remembered as having said, "Give me a place to stand, and I will move the Earth" when discussing the function and utility of levers. To move the data, we need a place beyond it. Sixteenth-century Europe is our place to stand. Let us go there and set up our heuristic tool, scripture, so that we might move on to moving the *Splendid Vision*.

SCRIPTURE IN CONTEXT

Scholars of religion generally date the inception of religious modernity to the year 1517, when Martin Luther initiated a battle over spiritual authority among Christianity's intellectual elite, and with it the Protestant Reformation. Prior to Martin Luther, western Christians were universally members of the Catholic Church, who acknowledged the authority of spiritual entities such as Jesus, the holy spirit, and the Bible. Nearly all also accepted the Catholic Church's ecclesiastical hierarchy—ranging from the pope, through the cardinals and bishops, to the parish priests—as the primary arbiter of spiritual authority on earth. Even mystics, individuals who felt themselves touched directly by Jesus himself, turned to priestly confessors in order to confirm the authenticity of their visions. From baptism at birth, through communion, to marriage and then death, Catholic doctrine held that no human being could lead a Christian, sacramental life without the direct intervention of the priestly order.

Though Martin Luther was hardly the first critic of clerical privilege, his were the first words to reach enough ears with sufficient force to split western Christianity in two. Luther's career as a reformer began in 1517 when he famously nailed a list of principles and accusations to the door of Wittenberg's Castle Church. This document—known as the 95 Theses—aired many grievances, two of which are fundamental to how we think about scripture today. On the one hand, Luther extolled biblical scripture as Christianity's singular authority. In his later writings, Luther expressed this principle in a ready catchphrase: *Sola scriptura*, literally, *Through scripture alone!* On the other hand, Luther impugned the papacy. By tradition, the pope was considered the highest earthly authority regarding matters of spirit. For Luther, however, Pope Leo X went too far. For in his view, the church under this pope acted as if the priestly power to grant indulgences was of greater significance than the gospels; and Luther likewise worried that the pope had arrogated powers to himself that must be reserved for god alone. Bible beats pope. The supersession of authority, from the human ecclesiastical hierarchy to the scriptural book, was the cornerstone of Christianity's Protestant Reformation.

For western Christians living before the sixteenth century, god could reveal his will through a multitude of means. To read god's mind, Christians looked to the forces of nature, the inner pangs of conscience, mystical visions, the institution and practices of the universal church, as well as to the scriptural word. Luther and other Protestant reformers, by contrast, referred all sources of knowledge concerning god, his will, or his providence to the category of scripture. "No believing Christian," Luther advised, "can be forced to recognize any authority beyond the sacred scripture."[9] Scripture deserved this singular preeminence because it alone was god's direct self-revelation. Luther's theology presented god as having two levels: one hidden, the other revealed. Luther characterized the hidden god as, "God as He is in His own nature and Majesty."[10] Like an iceberg, god's depths could not be known from looking at the surface. But whereas an oceanographer might use sounding technology to fathom an iceberg's hidden dimensions, Luther emphasized that human beings could *never* penetrate into the truths god had hidden. God's mysteries were for god alone. Anything a theologian might say about the hidden divinity would be wholly speculative and, as such, given the dignity of the topic ought not be said at all.

Instead, Luther entreated his readers to fix their gaze on divinity as it exists in the human world, namely the Bible. God revealed the word to human beings in order to allow us to know something of the divine nature, will, and plan. For postapostolic Christians, scriptural revelation remained the only definite means by which human beings could receive divine guidance in the art of being righteous. Hence Luther's dictum, *Sola scriptura!*

What does this have to do with the *Splendid Vision*? The present section builds, piece by piece, a generic model of *scripture* that I then use later in the essay, as a heuristic, to consider how the *Splendid Vision* works. Even though the word *scripture* is now used for texts and phenomena other than the Bible,[11] and even though writings that Luther or Calvin would have dismissed as pagan superstition—including the *Splendid Vision*—are now regularly included under this rubric, our contemporary usage is nevertheless deeply indebted to the reformers' singular passion for the biblical word.

What makes "scripture" scriptural? As I use the term, *scripturality* is defined by three generic characteristics. So far we have touched upon the first of the three. *As a genre, we find "scripture" where we find a text that a community accepts as possessed of exceptional, universal, or superhuman value.* Note, although a text may claim extraordinary value or supreme authority for itself—certainly this is true of the *Splendid Vision*—a text should be categorized as scripture proper only if people treat it as divinely revealed, transcendentally authored, intrinsically authoritative, or, simply, sacred. Scripturality describes, not the book itself, but a community's transactional relationship with the book.

To read the *Splendid Vision* as scripture, accordingly, requires that we pay attention to how members of a community—ancient or modern—might perceive and treat it as a source of exceptional, universal value. For our imaginative engagement with the past, we have Shulkshina and Shulivujna as the representatives of that community; for our imaginative engagement with the present, we have my tattooed student. But now we have to move on. For before we can return to the *Splendid Vision*, two more dimensions of scripturality must be gleaned from early Reformation discourse on the biblical word.

Let us turn to a verbal duel between a Catholic cardinal, Jacopo Sadoleto, and Jean Calvin, a Protestant reformer whose historical stature is equal to that of Martin Luther himself. Writing in 1539, each man is attempting to convince the other that his own form of Christianity is legitimate, while the other's is false religion. Thus Cardinal Sadoleto argues:

> The [Catholic] Church errs not, and even cannot err, since the Holy Spirit constantly guides her public and universal decrees and councils.[12]

Calvin retorts,

> Seeing how dangerous it would be to boast of the Spirit without the Word, He [God] declared the Church is indeed governed by the Holy Spirit, but in order that the government might not be vague and unstable, He annexed it to the Word. For this reason Christ exclaims that those who are of God hear the Word of God.[13]

Both men make fervent appeal to the holy spirit; both treat the holy spirit as legitimating human practice. For Sadoleto, the Catholic Church cannot err because the holy spirit—god himself—guides it directly, without intermediary. Calvin the reformer, by contrast, acknowledges the holy spirit's influence on the Church but proposes that all claims to spirit must be tested against the word. When the Church violates the word then it violates the spirit as well. Thus in the next paragraph, Calvin adds, "It is no less reasonable to boast of the Spirit without the Word than it would be absurd to bring forward the Word itself without the Spirit."[14] Word and spirit are not precisely the same, yet, for Calvin, they never exist apart from one another. A discussion of this simultaneity of word and spirit will clarify a second dimension of scripturality. The initial investigation into scripturality focused on the source and nature of scripture; this second highlights the matter of interpretation, that is, how scripture serves as a source of true knowledge.

Think about it: Sadoleto and Calvin both read the same Bible; both made appeal to the same holy spirit. How can they have held such divergent theological positions? The answer, of course, is that they did not read the same Bible, exactly, nor did they exactly appeal to the same holy spirit. For Sadoleto, the Bible was only one among many sources of continuing revelation; the spirit inhabited and illuminated institutions, traditions, holy relics, and other sacra as well as minds and hearts. For the man of *Sola scriptura* . . . well, the word *sola* does not leave much room for compromise. *Everything* god wants us to know about the spiritual realm—about him, about ourselves, about life and death, time and space—is present within the revealed word. The rest is impenetrable mystery. Thus, even the principles by which human beings read and interpret scripture are necessarily part of scripture itself. One must use scripture in order to interpret scripture.

Given that scripture is the only way to apprehend the divine, everything worth discovering is present therein. For the reformers, this principle entailed a revision of scriptural hermeneutics away from medieval paradigms. According to the simplest formulation, the Bible can be interpreted in one of two basic ways, either spiritually or literally.[15] Spiritual interpretations are characterized by some sort of referent beyond the immediate text. Thus, for instance, a spiritual reading of the Song of Songs would interpret this hymn from the Hebrew Bible—composed many centuries before Jesus' birth—as being about the tender relationship between Jesus Christ and his beloved Church. Reformers, like Luther and Calvin, rejected such spiritual approaches to reading the Bible. For them, the word of god was primarily a literal document. By *literal* they did not necessarily mean that every word in the Bible had to mean exactly what it said, and nothing more. They did allow that biblical writing could include figures of speech, idioms, and metaphors. Nevertheless, given that a good and loving god had inspired the book, it was only reasonable that divine revelation would be supremely revelatory. The Bible would present divine truths with utmost clarity and plainness. Thus, for Luther, *literal* meant everyday or commonplace: "Everywhere we should stick to just the simple, natural meaning of the words, as yielded by the rules of grammar and the habits of speech that God has created among men."[16] Confusions about the text, or seeming inconsistencies, or difficult phrases: these were matters for philology not theology. Approached in this way, Luther writes, "The literal sense of Scripture alone is the whole essence of faith and of Christian theology."[17]

This brings us back to the holy spirit. Throughout much of Christian history, literal and spiritual interpretations of scripture went hand in hand. Educated priests and writers delighted in interpreting the divine word as allegory. The Protestant reformers' intense stress on biblical literalism, on the overtness and clarity of the text, was, thus, a radical hermeneutic innovation. It was grounded, in part, in their theory of divine hiddenness and revelation: spiritual, allegorical readings of the text would sinfully tear away the curtain of mystery surrounding the hidden god. Thus they condemned a millennium of religious scholarship as sinful and debased. Beyond this, however, the reformers also allowed that it is neither easy nor simple to see what is right before one's eyes. Yes, the Bible is plain and clear, but unless one is touched by the holy spirit one will remain in darkness. As Luther wrote:

> The truth is that nobody who has not the Spirit of God sees a jot of what is in the Scriptures. All men have their hearts darkened, so that, even when they can discuss and quote all that is in Scripture, they do not understand or really know any of it. . . . The Spirit is needed for the understanding of all Scripture and every part of Scripture. . . . [Yet, if one does have the Spirit,] all that is in the Scripture is through the Word brought forth into the clearest light and proclaimed to the whole world.[18]

If many centuries of churchmen had not *really* seen scripture for what it was, the answer lay in the explanation that they had not been properly enlightened by the holy spirit. Those whose hearts and minds have been touched by the holy spirit, by contrast, will receive his word with proper faith. In one of the nicer ironies from this period, Protestant reformers held that, in order to read scripture literally, one had to be in a state of spiritual grace.

Early in this essay, I used the phrase sleight of hand to describe a situation wherein scholars appear to treat ideas as if they have a life apart from human beings, granting ideas a logical priority over the people who may actually think them. This inversion allows scholars to treat people as if they are mere agents of ideas; as if they can actually know what is going on inside an individual by reading a scholastic exposition of her avowed belief system. The sleight of hand lies in the scholarly expectation that books are reliable when people are not, even though, of course, books do not write themselves.

Here we see a parallel situation. In this case, the trick is that members of a scriptural community regard their authoritative texts as elementally true and infallible, even though they always read those texts interpretively, and thus treat them as fallible. The tension between scriptural infallibility and interpretation is clear in some instances. Clearly, a believer who accepts modern cosmology and evolutionary theory will have to jump through interpretive hoops in order to make Genesis's account of creation harmonize with empirical science. Clearly, a Christian for whom Jesus is the Prince of Peace will need an interpretive schema to justify Matthew 10:34's statement that Jesus does not bring peace, but a sword. Interpretation mediates, and harmonizes, expectations of scripture's inerrant facticity with the community's extrascriptural knowledge and expectations about the world.

A parallel dynamic is present in the case of Luther and Calvin as well, but with a twist. Luther and Calvin do not interpret the Bible by rephrasing its difficult passages in less-difficult terms. They interpret it by letting it speak plainly in its own, sometimes astounding, voice. On the face of it, this kind of literal reading would seem to be noninterpretive; it would seem that neither Luther nor Calvin brings any kind of personal bias to his understanding. And yet, both men justify their biblical literalism by reference to an extrascriptural theology of divine grace: no man, for them, can read the Bible literally unless he is enlightened by god. So, to read the Bible literally requires no less of an interpretive framework than to read it in harmony with evolutionary theory or a theology of peace. It's just that Luther and Calvin, like stage magicians, hide their interpretive framework in plain sight.

Here, then, is the second dimension of scripturality to be brought to bear upon the sutra: *as a genre, we find "scripture" where we find a text that a community accepts as an authoritative source of information, and that the community interprets in order to maintain for itself the perception of the source's elemental accuracy.* Scriptural authority may pertain to information about the natural world or the supernatural world, to morality or ritual, to social relations or individual desires, to this life or the next. No specific subject matter is either necessary or excluded. What *is* required here is that members of the community take the text's testimony as justified and correct, even when it contradicts their own empirical experience. And again, since contradictions are inevitable, members of the community will invoke some form of interpretive schema—whether literary, philological, historical, or theological—in order to close the cognitive gap. The claim that one must be illumined or enlightened to have eyes to see scripture's plain truth is fundamentally an interpretive claim.

To apply this second dimension of scripturality to the *Splendid Vision* we will want to pay attention to how the sutra represents itself as the direct embodiment of an enlightened spirit, with special insight into the nature of reality. Now for scripturality's third dimension.

"All men have their hearts darkened," Martin Luther writes, "so that, even when they discuss and quote all that is in Scripture, they do not understand or really know any of it." Likewise for Jean Calvin, scripture is "wrapped in enigmas" for those from whom god keeps his spirit, so that they may be cast "into greater stupidity."[19] Thus, we come to the third dimension of scripturality. Namely, scripture is existentially fraught. Some people have been enlightened; others remain in the dark. Some accept a specific work as capital-*S* scripture; others do not. Some are able to read scripture literally, as a plain revelation of ultimacy; others find casuistry, complexity, or cleverness. For Protestant reformers, these were not simply matters of personal preference. An individual's position on one side of these oppositions, or the other, was an indication of his state of grace; his faith in god; his salvation. Somebody who recognized the innate authority of the Bible and who, in turn, took its words as literal truths was illuminated by the holy spirit, and saved. Somebody who scoffed at this literalism and read the Bible allegorically or as mystical document, or worse yet, somebody who did not even accept the biblical word as revelation, was deranged by god. For such a person, the reformers could only imagine an eternity of brimstone.

To complete our model of scripturality: *as a genre, we find "scripture" where we find a text that a community expects to be performed, not just read or heard.* The word *performed* here does not mean using the scripture as a script in a formal context, like a ritual or dramatic theater. Quite the contrary: the most common context for scriptural performance is the day-to-day life of a human being. The second generic property of scripture entails interpretation of a cognitive nature. Likewise this dimension entails interpreting a text, albeit through physical action. To "perform" scripture means to accept its authority and let its words govern the unfolding moments of one's life. Extending this principle, we may add that *we find "scripture" where we find a text that a community treats as existentially fraught.* Scriptures have power for their communities, such that adhering to, or violating, them is believed to hold profound consequences in this world and the next. To grasp how the *Splendid Vision* works as scripture requires us to pay attention to how this sutra's audience may have used it. Let us also attend to how they might have judged the *Splendid Vision*'s threats and promises: threats against those who would disparage or dismiss its teachings; promises of boundless prosperity to those who would accept it on its own terms.

As a heuristic model, in sum, scripturality has three generic properties. We find "scripture" where we find a text that a community treats as

1. *possessed of exceptional, universal, or superhuman value;*

2. *an authoritative source of information about the world, interpreting that source as needed in order to maintain the perception of its elemental accuracy;*
3. *existentially fraught, that is, they expect it to be performed, not just read or heard.*

The first property pertains to the value placed on scripture. The second property pertains to scripture as a source of truth, bringing together information and interpretation. The third property pertains to using scripture as a guide to action and the consequences thereof. A text becomes a scripture when people treat it as an authoritative source of value, truth, and meaning.

Traces of early Protestant theology linger in our words when we categorize the *Splendid Vision* as scripture. Although the preceding paragraphs speak a great deal about god and spirit, the important lesson to take from this discussion is anthropological, not theological. Luther's and Calvin's theological interest in scriptural revelation also concomitantly formulated a theory of who and what we are as human beings. It is this anthropic twist to revealed scripture that we bring to bear on the *Splendid Vision*.

As a term in Protestant anthropology, *scripture* provides a means for imagining the categorical divide between divinity and humanity. In this relationship, god alone plays an active role. He inspires and inhabits the body of scripture; he gives humanity the means to understand and follow it; and he judges whether we have responded to his revelation with righteousness. Human beings, by contrast, are characterized by receptivity and submission. We accept the word as divinely revealed; we read the word following divine intentions; and we strive to follow the word in everything we do. This is what it means to be a human being in a world created by the kind of god who requires us to approach him through scripture alone.

Naturally, when we investigate the *Splendid Vision* in terms of this heuristic model of scripturality, much will change. Beyond a switch to Sanskrit, Indian Buddhism's cosmology, elaboration of the superhuman and supernatural, mechanisms of enlightenment, as well as its ideal for human life are vastly different from those of the sixteenth-century Christian reformers. Nevertheless, what remains the same across continents, centuries, and religions is that we read Buddhist sutras as scripture, just as we read the Bible as scripture, in order to learn about being human. For the *Splendid Vision*, members of its audience exist, not in a universe created by god ex nihilo, but rather in a cosmos inhabited by other beings who have taken vows to become buddhas for the sake of every sentient creature, and in which some indeed have succeeded in perfecting that vow. Let us now enter that cosmos, bringing with us a heightened attention to the three elements of scripturality.

The *Splendid Vision* as Scripture: Setting the Scene

THUS HAVE I HEARD

"Thus have I heard" (§1). The *Splendid Vision* begins thusly, as does nearly every sutra in the Buddhist corpus. Sutras open with this affirmation for a number of reasons. Like the "Once upon a time" of fairy tales, these words prepare an audience to receive the narrative that follows in an appropriate state of mind. When a dharma preacher announced, "Thus have I heard," some members of his audience readied themselves, straightening their backs and stilling their thoughts, while others perhaps welcomed the opportunity for a stolen nap. Beyond marking a text's genre or initiating its oral performance, however, the affirmation "Thus have I heard" also spoke to the sutra's authenticity as a revelation of dharma. It bespoke a line of transmission stretching back to Shakyamuni himself. The purpose of such a guarantee cuts to the heart of Buddhism as a religion, and thus to that of the *Splendid Vision* as a scripture.

Doctrinally, Buddhism presupposes parity between the outer and the inner worlds. The more fully an individual comprehends the objective truth, the nearer she approaches the end of subjective suffering. Every living being has the capacity to realize enlightenment and thus attain nirvana's peace. However, as the *Splendid Vision* laments, most people get it backwards. In order to forestall pain, they fill their time with "eating, drinking, joking, and dancing" (§48), propelling themselves ever further from lasting satisfaction. Such frivolities may bring a sense of liberty and ease for a moment, but in the long run they bring only greater bondage. To win enduring freedom, individuals must heed discourses like the *Splendid Vision*, which "guarantee that the tathagata's teachings persevere for the benefit of all beings" (§113). Yet, why would somebody who enjoys bodily pleasures renounce sweet delight on the advice of the *Splendid Vision* unless she were to be convinced that the sutra offers still more rarified satisfactions? And even if the *Splendid Vision* promises to give her everything she can imagine, why should she trust it? Why believe that it is filled with the practical insights of someone who actually tasted purest freedom? Why accept it as authoritative? This need for a seal of authenticity was solved, in part, by the opening phrase, "Thus have I heard."[20] Here we touch the first dimension of scripturality, extraordinary value. To grasp how four commonplace words might transform a story into a scripture requires some background in Buddhist history and principles.

After Shakyamuni's death, monks were concerned to preserve his teachings with close precision. Likewise, they hoped to maintain harmony in their small community. As you might imagine, these two desires were not always easy to reconcile, since points of doctrine are open to divergent interpretations, leading to irresolvable arguments, resulting in bitter schisms. The *Mahaparinirvana Sutra*, a scripture telling of Shakyamuni's final days, offers ample evidence of these concerns. Near this sutra's beginning, the buddha teaches seven ways to ensure institutional longevity, instructing his assembly how to survive after his death and flourish despite his absence. For each of the seven points, collective unanimity is the key to success. As evidence that harmony is an attainable ideal, just before Shakyamuni dies his friend Ananda observes that his followers are perfectly schooled: "Not a single monk in the assembly has any doubt, any uncertainty."[21] Thus tradition teaches that when the buddha entered complete and final nirvana, his disciples were of one mind and one spirit, unanimous and harmonious through their shared understanding of dharma. Indeed, the sutra offers a brief commentary on the peace of Shakyamuni's deathbed tableau: "This has been done by the Tathagata for the sake of those people who will follow hereafter."[22]

In truth, the people who followed thereafter required something more than just this scene recorded in the *Mahaparinirvana Sutra*. They required a comprehensive strategy for enforcing unanimity and preserving harmony. At the heart of that strategy was a story: the story of the First Council, a convocation of five hundred arhats who gathered in the Indian town of Rajgir just months after Shakyamuni's death. As arhats, these men were considered profoundly wise and incapable of harboring ulterior motives. The group spent several months collectively recollecting every word Shakyamuni had spoken during his forty-five years as a wandering sage. For contemporary scholars the historicity of the First Council as an actual event is open to debate. Nevertheless, the traditional value of the council as myth appertaining to institutional self-regulation is clear. Throughout their history, Buddhists have been able to affirm that, soon after Shakyamuni's death, his doctrines and rules of conduct were recited in full and confirmed as the legitimate "word of buddha" by a congregation of five hundred bright, generous, and completely trustworthy men, all of whom had personally heard the buddha teach. The First Council provided a welcome touchstone for a community that prized unity but lacked a single acknowledged leader. In Shakyamuni's absence, there could be one community sharing one scriptural canon.

Legend has it that Ananda, the buddha's closest friend and constant companion, played a crucial role at this First Council. Ananda is the "I" of "Thus have I heard," for it was Ananda who recollected and recited Shakyamuni's sutras in front of the five hundred assembled monks. Ananda was given this privilege because, in the words of a later commentary, "among the buddha's disciples, [Ananda] served the buddha every day and was seen close to the buddha. He heard the texts, was able to remember them, and the buddha constantly praised and approved of him."[23] Ananda, in short, was always in the right place at the right time. Moreover, Ananda had one more factor in his favor: Shakyamuni Buddha's own stamp of approval.

To see how Shakyamuni so valued Ananda, let us return to the *Splendid Vision*, jumping to the conclusion. By opening "Thus have I heard," the *Splendid Vision* marks itself as a Buddhist sutra. No other genre of literature begins in just this way. Authored perhaps one millennium after Shakyamuni's death, the *Splendid Vision* preserves the enduring image of Ananda as having memorized the buddha's every spoken word. Of course, metaphors, icons, and stories often lose their affective force over the centuries, becoming dull clichés. This is not the case with Ananda in the *Splendid Vision*. The sutra does not just passively rely on the general value of memories regarding Ananda or the First Council as a kind of authenticating capital. Rather, the sutra uses Ananda as an active character, in order to win its audience's loyalty. For Ananda differs from Avalokiteshvara, Manjushri, the buddha, the yakshinis—all the other active performers in the *Splendid Vision*'s drama—in that, within the Mahayana literary universe, he plays the role of a mere human being. Ananda is a better man than you or I, perhaps, but he often functions in Mahayana sutras as an "everyman" character, an individual with whom members of the sutra's audience can personally identify. With this in mind, we read at the sutra's end:

> Then venerable Ananda spoke, "Blessed lord, I accept this dharma discourse. Regarding this dharma discourse as my teacher, I will preserve it, worship it, and make it known it to all beings." (§107)

Here Ananda proclaims his enthusiasm for the *Splendid Vision* as well as his determination to make it available after Shakyamuni's death. But in the words of the sutra, these gestures alone are insufficient. Shakyamuni demands more of Ananda and, by extension, of the sutra's audience. For as the buddha explains, the *Splendid Vision* is the unparalleled gem of the Buddhist canon. The seriousness of the situation here is marked by the fact that Shakyamuni does not merely instruct Ananda; he also threatens his friend (in keeping with the third dimension of scripturality). If Ananda fails to memorize the *Splendid Vision*, Shakyamuni will demote his companion and end the close friendship that is the source of Ananda's prestige and joy:

> Ananda, suppose you fail to preserve, recite, worship, or disseminate the totality of my dharma teachings which you have heard and remembered. In that case, you would not offend me and would not have disobeyed me. I would still consider you my disciple. Now suppose you fail to preserve, recite, worship, disseminate, or remember this dharma discourse. In that case, you would offend me and have disobeyed me. You would no longer be my disciple. (§108)

Since you are reading this book, clearly Ananda did not fail.

The *Splendid Vision*'s opening phrase, "Thus have I heard," aligns the text nicely with our generic model of scripture. Before a member of the sutra's audience would accept its particular explication of the cosmic order (scriptural dimension no. 2: truth) or quiver at its threats and exalt in its promises (scriptural dimension no. 3: existential meaning), that audience member had to accept the sutra as a genuine expression of dharma (scriptural dimension no. 1: value). Again and again the *Splendid Vision* makes absolute claims for its own extraordinary, universal value and significance: Beings are definitely liberated from old age, disease, and death after they "hear this dharma discourse, after they worship it and disseminate it, after they consider its meaning and practice its practices" (§98). Again and again the sutra tells its audience to look to its pages for the truth: that truth being that one should prize the *Splendid Vision* above all else because it contains the truth. By beginning the text "Thus have I heard," the *Splendid Vision*'s author sought to convince at least part of its audience to take this claim to heart.

THE GREAT ASSEMBLY ON POTALAKA MOUNTAIN

Now exercise your imagination. It is the fifteenth day of the month, the full-moon day, the day on which Shulkshina and Shulivujna regularly invite a dharma preacher to their home. Fine rugs and cushions soften their courtyard dirt. Wisps of exotic sandalwood smoke rise and spread, as Shulkshina and Shulivujna sing in praise of the three jewels. Perhaps these devotees know the title of today's sutra, perhaps not. Either way, when the preacher begins, "Thus have I heard," their bodies thrill with anticipation. The "I" erases the thousand years between Shulkshina and Shulivujna's era and that of Ananda. These words transform a thousand-mile journey into a single short step.

Ananda's first-person testimony—voiced by the preacher—transports Shulkshina and Shulivujna directly to the buddha's side. Now Shulkshina and Shulivujna are not simply in Shakyamuni's presence, they are also in his world: the world of dharma, where the rhythms of space and time are nothing like those of our default world. So let us consider the sutra's set and setting. Historian Brian Galloway observes that, following the phrase "Thus have I heard," "Buddhist tradition required that 'place and time' be stated at the beginning of a sutra as evidence of its authenticity."[24] Beyond mere literary conventions, however, time and space are the contextual dimensions of human life. Beginning with our physical bodies pulled hard to earth, we cannot even begin to cognize or experience the world without orienting our ideas and experiences in spatial and temporal terms. Lacking these four dimensions, you are not you and I am not I.

It is hardly surprising that considerations of space and time are integral to the articulation of scripture. For it is difficult to see how individuals like Shulkshina and Shulivujna could have accepted the *Splendid Vision* as extraordinarily and universally valuable (scripturality no. 1, value) unless they simultaneously regarded the sutra as a source of privileged insight into the transcendental factors of human experience (scripturality no. 2, truth). Add to this the fact that the *Splendid*

Vision is so thoroughly engrossed in an active rhetoric of self-autho-rization—claiming again and again to manifest the very truth that it teaches—and we should likewise not be astonished that the sutra pres-ents itself, spatially and temporally, as a world unto itself.

How does this differ from *The Twilight Zone*? Recall the show's introduction: "You're traveling through another dimension, a dimen-sion not only of sight and sound but of mind; a journey into a won-drous land whose boundaries are that of imagination." Community, of course, is the factor dividing scripture from popular fantasy. Like the TV show, the *Splendid Vision* makes almost boundless claims regard-ing the malleability of space and time. But for this text to be scripture, it simultaneously requires the presence of a community whose mem-bers accept the sutra's cosmic map as more completely true and more definitively real than the rutted trails of their everyday experience, no matter how widely the two may diverge. In fact, in accord with scrip-turality element no. 3 (existential meaning), the *Splendid Vision* even offers people like Shulkshina and Shulivujna a way to transport them-selves from one world to the other, from their dull everyday lives to the sutra's parallel cosmos of spiritual delight.

To clarify this point, let us return briefly to the example of Chris-tianity. Protestant reformers argued that, as scripture, the Bible must be read literally, in its plainest sense. If the Old Testament claims that Jehovah created human beings, first Adam, then Eve, then this is how our species came to be on earth. If the New Testament claims that Jesus raised Lazarus from the dead, and later rose himself, then Jesus did indeed conquer death. Even though the Bible presents infor-mation that exceeds human experience and capabilities for knowing, concerning events that violate the normal workings of time, space, and existence, the reformers directed their followers to take the Bible at its word. Indeed, they proposed that the willingness to accept scrip-ture's most counterintuitive and irrational claims literally, as unques-tioned truths, is proof that one has been graced by the holy spirit. Only deranged empiricists, abandoned by god, would value the testimony of their own senses over that of scripture. Lacking the touch of spirit, one simply lacks the faculties needed to perceive the scripture, and the world, as they *truly* are.

The *Splendid Vision* does not use the same wording as the Protestant reformers. It does not speak of its particular reality as "literal." Nor does it direct its audience to read its plain sense. Nevertheless, the *Splendid Vision*'s introduction does work toward a parallel purpose, and may profitably be considered within the heuristic ambit of scripturality's second dimension, truth. At the sutra's beginning and end, Avalokiteshvara exclaims that, for the tathagata, "nothing is unseen, unheard, or unknown" (§§16, 97). If, like the Bible, the *Splendid Vision* describes happenings that bend space and suspend time, it is only because Shakyamuni exists within a *realer* reality. Ananda's "Thus have I heard"—linked to the legend of the First Council—is only one of many strategies this sutra's author uses to entice his audience to take its statements at face value, despite the fact that they contravene everyday experience and common sense. Let us now return to the sutra for parallel examples.

"At one time the blessed lord was staying at the home of noble Avalokiteshvara on Potalaka Mountain" (§1). Here we have the rudiments of the *Splendid Vision*'s space-time coordinates. The temporal assertion "at one time" reminds us again of the fairy tale's "Once upon a time." However, the "Once upon a time" of fairy tales distances listeners from what they hear, aesthetically and temporally; the past it creates is fully passed. The sutra, by contrast, does not create so determinate a sense of temporality. For the sutra pairs its imprecise marker of time, "at one time," with a precise marker of identity, the "I" of "Thus have I heard." Thus it seems as if this sutra, recited at no specific time, is always recited as if for the first time, even right now.

Like time, space has moods. Space, as found in a Buddhist sutra, is not like the space of mathematics and physics. Geometrical space is supposed to be perfectly regular, with the same laws working in the same way everywhere. Buddhist space, by contrast, allows that some places are more spiritually charged than others. In the language of the *Splendid Vision*, some pieces of ground are worthy of worship, while others are not. Just as the *Splendid Vision* accomplishes its goals by playing with normal perceptions of mundane temporality, so the articulation of alternative notions of spatial existence is critical to the *Splendid Vision*'s cosmogonic project.

The *Splendid Vision* begins to create this world, as do other Buddhist sutras, by giving a detailed description of the place where Shakyamuni spoke, as well as of the manifold entities who gathered there to hear him. The *Splendid Vision* was presented atop Potalaka Mountain, the sylvan abode of the bodhisattva Avalokiteshvara. In contemporary scholarship, Avalokiteshvara is often characterized as a mythological personage, and his home, Potalaka Mountain, can likewise be deemed a mythological location. This use of *myth* requires clarification.

Myths are a privileged class of narratives or declarative statements that, in the words of literary critic Roland Barthes, have "the task of giving an historical intention a natural justification, and making contingency appear eternal."[25] In other words, myths are stories that represent the exact concerns of a specific group of people in such a way as to represent the universe itself as structured by those concerns. For instance, we call Avalokiteshvara a mythological bodhisattva because, on the one hand, historians have established the approximate century in which the personage of Avalokiteshvara was first invented and the historical contingencies of that invention.[26] Outsiders and nonbelievers would view Avalokiteshvara as neither more real nor more imaginary a personage than Superman. Yet on the other hand, countless people over the millennia have been convinced of Avalokiteshvara's beneficent existence and regulated their behaviors based upon that conviction. Insiders and believers intone, "Om Mani Padme Hum, Om Mani Padme Hum," for the sutras teach that Avalokiteshvara will not allow misfortune to strike anyone who chants his mantra. For them, we live in the kind of cosmos in which Avalokiteshvara as the bodhisattva of compassion makes sense.

The categories of myth and scripture overlap conceptually. A scripture is a text that a community accepts as elementally true and thus, with proper interpretation, as an infallible source of information. Myth, by extension, is the specific information recorded in scripture. Thus to rephrase my presentation of scripture in the earlier section: when people interpret scriptures in order to harmonize scriptural claims with their expectations and experiences, they are more properly interpreting myth. No matter the terminology, however, in order to understand both scripture and myth we have to foreground the question of social groupings. In the case of a given text—the *Splendid Vision*, for instance—we will speak of the text as scripture, or not, and speak of its content as myth, or not, depending upon the social group whose perspective is being considered. A text can be true *and* false, infallible *and* gibberish, scripture *and* fiction, a teacher of myth *and* a source of nonsense, simultaneously. Scriptures define and distinguish communities. Buddhists regard myths about Avalokiteshvara as information that may save their lives, while I may consider those same myths to be fabrications and wish-fulfillment fantasies. Using the term *myth* helps to highlight the way in which the reception of scriptural content devolves into social identities: they are Mahayana Buddhists; I am a secular academic.

Among Mahayana Buddhism's mythological bodhisattvas, Avalokiteshvara was certainly the most popular and most prevalent. In particular, Avalokiteshvara was conceived as a savior. His name translating literally as The Lord Who Looked Down, Avalokiteshvara worked marvels. Once, it is said, he saved thousands of worms from suffering by taking the form of a bee and buzzing the formula for refuge in the three jewels so that the worms could gain insight and merit. Another time, he became a flying horse and rescued shipwrecked merchants from an island of ogresses. Of course, Avalokiteshvara was also credited with far more mundane acts of assistance—pacifying venomous snakes, easing the pains of childbirth, soothing the egos of cruel tyrants.[27]

When Avalokiteshvara was not thus occupied, he dwelt on Potalaka, a mountain near India's southern tip. As Xuanzang, the renowned seventh-century Chinese traveler and translator, describes it:

Potalaka Mountain has perilous paths and precipitous cliffs and valleys. On top of the mountain is a lake of clear water, issuing in a big river that flows twenty times around the mountain before passing into the South Sea. Beside the lake is a stone heavenly palace which is frequented by Avalokiteshvara Bodhisattva. Those who wish to see the Bodhisattva risk their lives to cross the river and climb up the mountain, regardless of hardship and danger, but only a few of them reach their destination.[28]

Though quite detailed, these words from Xuanzang's travelogue are fanciful. Yes, we can find Potalaka on a map: Potiyil Mountain, near the town of Ambasamudram in the modern Indian state of Tamil Nadu.[29] Potalaka is nevertheless a mythic place, for its place in the *Splendid Vision* is not a function of its longitude and latitude. What matters is that the *Splendid Vision*'s opening phrases work to move its audience's minds and hearts, if not their bodies, to a mountain steeped in dharma, possessing a rough beauty, looming over the far edge of the Indian subcontinent. If we think of space and time as existential coordinates, the *Splendid Vision* becomes accepted as scripture to the degree that a community feels—knows—the mythic world it describes to be more substantial than that of their daily drudge.

The congregation that gathered at Potalaka to witness the *Splendid Vision* was likewise appropriate to this mythic abode. Shakyamuni, seated on a royal throne draped with flowers and gems, was surrounded by monks, bodhisattvas, laymen, laywomen, gods, nagas, gandharvas, yakshinis, and all the deities who guard the world. This is a typical audience for a Mahayana sutra. Indeed, like Ananda's "I" and the stipulation of a place and time for the sutra's articulation, the claim that Shakyamuni's audience included many types of entities is a generic property of Mahayana sutra literature. Within the common Buddhist cosmology, gods, nagas, and other such superhuman beings are not supernatural. They range beyond humanity in terms of the scope of their abilities and the fullness of their pleasures, but what they do and what they enjoy remain fully within the realm of what we call *nature*.

More important, the *Splendid Vision*'s congregation is marked by the superiority of its members' spiritual attainments (§§2–7). Among the human beings present, for instance, the monks were all arhats, free of desires and possessing perfect control over their minds. Although these arhats had not pursued the more exalted path of a bodhisattva, within the limited ambit of their spiritual aspirations they were perfect. Similarly the laymen and laywomen present were not neophytes, hearing a sutra for the first time. How could such people have surmounted the dangers of Potalaka's slopes? To the contrary, these men and women all were human bodhisattvas capable (in our terms) of intergalactic travel through the force of their own minds. All these lay bodhisattvas had nearly completed their training for buddhahood: buddhas had told them so and buddhas do not lie. Although these laymen and laywomen were experts on the bodhisattva path, the sutra distinguishes them from "bodhisattvas" proper in order to suggest that the laity present at the *Splendid Vision*'s recitation on Potalaka did not look any different from Shulkshina or Shulivujna, or you or me. This destabilizes our usual snap judgments about people. Common-seeming folk might really be powerful bodhisattvas. What do you truly know about the bagger at the grocery store? Does every item she puts in the bag silently rescue another sentient being from samsara? Still more, what do you truly know about yourself and your own deep spiritual state? In his Potalaka home, Avalokiteshvara was only one among a company of what we might call cosmic bodhisattvas: mythological beings close to the final attainment of full and perfect buddhahood, who play a variety of roles in the literatures of Mahayana Buddhism. Vajrapani and Manjushri are two other well-known cosmic bodhisattvas who feature prominently in the sutra. Finally, other members of the *Splendid Vision*'s audience included various deities associated in the Indian pantheon with earth, water, sky, and the starry heavens above.

SHAKYAMUNI'S *SON ET LUMIÈRE*

The *Splendid Vision* may readily be redescribed in terms of scripture and myth. The sutra's introduction displays a panoply of beings arriving at Potalaka Mountain from all the higher realms of embodied existence. The gathering included superior humans, resplendent gods, theriomorphic spirits, and chthonic deities. All were champions of dharma; most were expert in dharma. All the very best beings in the universe were present on Potalaka Mountain to witness the buddha's preaching of the *Splendid Vision*, the very best discourse. As myth, moreover, the *Splendid Vision* arranges space in a hierarchical fashion, by articulating a distinction between presence and absence. It separates those who were capable of being present on Potalaka at that special time from those who lacked the prerequisite spiritual attainments or superhuman powers. But the *Splendid Vision* should not be considered myth simply because it divides living beings into one or more hierarchies. A business's institutional flowchart does the same. The term *myth* is useful because it reminds us to think about how the sutra's audience may have received and reacted to its elaboration of cosmic hierarchies. To the degree that Shulkshina and Shulivujna worried about or wondered where they fit into that cosmos, we can speak of the *Splendid Vision*'s introductory phrases as expressing a living myth. By definition, myths are never universally accepted; scriptures are always divisive texts. According to the *Splendid Vision*'s scriptural logic, you as a reader should feel anxious that you were not worthy to be present on Potalaka; or failing that, you should feel anxious that you do not feel anxious enough. That is the double bind of religion: the less you care, the worse you should feel.

At this point in the sutra's introduction, the *Splendid Vision*'s cosmogonic project is only half complete. In fact, from Shulkshina's and Shulivujna's perspective, this analysis, which claims that the *Splendid Vision* fashions a cosmos by perfectly expressing hierarchical values, may be said to grossly misrepresent the sutra as well as their religion. Throughout the *Splendid Vision* we find affirmations that all beings— not just a limited elite—will benefit from its teachings, practices, and presence. Thus near the sutra's end, Avalokiteshvara exclaims that the *Splendid Vision* "is proclaimed to all beings for a great purpose" (§104); while earlier in the text, Avalokiteshvara instructs readers to share their roots of virtue with all beings and fill their hearts with universal benevolence, sympathy, and compassion (§59). Likewise, Mahayana scholastic literature consistently emphasizes that religious people who have not become bodhisattvas "practice out of self-interest, while bodhisattvas practice from self-interest as well as a concern for others."[30] A twelfth-century initiation ritual takes this logic to its limit, directing bodhisattvas to eliminate the emotional distance between themselves and others by regarding all living beings as their own family members. A bodhisattva should vow: "I adopt the realm of infinite beings as my mother, father, sisters, brothers, sons, daughters, and every one of my other relatives and kinsmen."[31] How could such a bodhisattva possibly exclude others or create social divisions?

For answers, let us return to the *Splendid Vision*. After the sutra describes the congregation that gathered on Potalaka, it shifts focus to Shakyamuni. Although only superior individuals could make their way into his presence through their own efforts, the buddha was capable of bringing all other living beings to Potalaka as well. How did he accomplish this? The sutra explains:

> Then, at that time, the blessed lord entered into a samadhi named *abiding in the knowledge of great compassion, which takes all beings as its object of contemplation*. Through the power of that samadhi, this universe of three-thousand many-thousand worlds was filled with light. Once the whole universe was aglow, the blind could see. The deaf could hear. The sick became healthy. The naked were clothed. The mad gained their sanity. . . . Everybody was full of joy and their hopes were totally fulfilled. Inspired, every living being in this universe of three-thousand many-thousand worlds approached the blessed lord to hear the dharma. (§§9–10)

The cause-and-effect process is straightforward, if not simple. The buddha enters into a samadhi, which fills the universe with light, which pleases and satisfies all beings, which inspires them to pay attention to the dharma, which attracts them to the buddha.

To start this chain reaction, Shakyamuni enters into a *samadhi*. This Sanskrit term plays a critical role in the *Splendid Vision* and requires our close attention. *The Treasury of Higher Learning*, an influential fifth-century textbook on Buddhist doctrine, defines *samadhi* as "one-pointedness of thought," and then explains: "Samadhi occurs when the mind becomes continuously fixed on a single object though meditation [*yoga*]."[32] Given this definition, it is not surprising that samadhi has been translated into English as concentration, trance, meditative concentration, and mental absorption. Every one of these terms or phrases suggests that samadhi is internal, mental, and stable; a state achieved through the strenuous effort of fixing the mind upon its own interior objects and processes. This accords with the word *samadhi*'s root significance: "putting together," "combining," or "arranging." A mind in samadhi is composed and orderly. Note, however, *The Treasury of Higher Learning*'s commentary distinguishes samadhi from the yogic practice of meditation itself. In common usage, meditation is a technique for restraining or directing the mind. Samadhi, by contrast, is the content that fills the mind when meditative techniques are properly applied.

Because samadhi is a matter of content rather than technique, it is not singular. Manuals of Buddhist meditation do not typically induce their readers into a unitary state of catatonic nothingness. Quite the contrary, the techniques of Buddhist meditation are dynamic. They train practitioners to cultivate a discerning perspective, a way of attending to the world that accords with dharma. Though this mental activity is not necessarily discursive (i.e., it does not follow a chain of words or images, as does ordinary thought), samadhi does, nonetheless, alter the way one apprehends the world. For this reason, my prior characterization of samadhi as "internal" is only half correct. Buddhist sources display ambivalence about whether meditation is just a matter of mind. Meditative states, samadhis plural, are often mapped onto cosmological states. A meditator can move around the cosmos, from earth to heaven or hell, mentally, by entering into specific states of samadhi. For example, one of the other texts unearthed at Gilgit tells a story in which Shakyamuni's disciple Maudgalyayana descends to the deepest hell, Avici, by descending into the proper samadhi. In

Avici, Maudgalyayana comforts the buddha's cousin, Devadatta, by informing him that he will be liberated in the far future.[33] Elsewhere, Maudgalyayana attains a specific samadhi so that he can ascend to heaven, to converse with Shakyamuni, who is spending his summer vacation among the gods.[34] More generally, Buddhist cosmologies describe "three realms": a realm of desire, a form realm, and a formless realm. As Rupert Gethin explains,

> At the heart of Buddhist thought . . . [there is] a basic ambiguity about matters of cosmology and psychology, about the objective outer world and the subjective inner world. This is true to the extent that the key to understanding both is a fundamental and profound equivalence between cosmology and psychology.[35]

Samadhi is so crucial to Buddhism because it provides the nexus, the locus of equivalence, between the inner and outer worlds.

Let us now return to the *Splendid Vision*'s description of Shakyamuni as entering into a samadhi named *abiding in the knowledge of great compassion, which takes all beings as its object of contemplation* (§9). Given the preceding paragraph, one might wonder whether this samadhi names a particular locale in the Buddhist universe. Does it name a heaven in the desire realm, perhaps? The answer is more complicated than that. The relatively simple system, whereby subjective internal states of meditative samadhi are directly correlated to objective external domains within the cosmos, is characteristic of non-Mahayana Buddhism. The great textbooks of the non-Mahayana sects provide gazetteers to a coherent and concrete cosmic structure. The expansion of the Mahayana saw profound shifts in Buddhism's emphases, ideals, truths, values, and practices. These changes redounded to the use of the term *samadhi* as well. Whereas in non-Mahayana Buddhism, samadhi ambiguously refers to mental states and cosmological locales within a well-defined order, for the Mahayana samadhis not only transport a bodhisattva or buddha around the cosmos but they also actually restructure the cosmos, or create an alternative one.

The words of Luis Gómez clarify how the term *samadhi* is being used in Mahayana sutras like the *Splendid Vision*. For the Mahayana, samadhi is

> a process that displays . . . before the eyes of the meditator, extraordinary worlds of visionary grandeur. The meditator can "open up" or "display" these visions for others, who then share in the meditator's experience, perceiving it as a sort of revelation.[36]

This is just what happens in the *Splendid Vision*. The buddha places himself in a cognitive state charged with the emotion of great compassion for all living beings; great compassion is, technically, the acceptance of responsibility to liberate all beings from suffering. Because of the slippage between inner and outer worlds, Shakyamuni's fixation upon great compassion transforms the universe itself. The *Splendid Vision* signals this transformation through its description of light shooting forth from Shakyamuni, filling the entire universe. Light carries a rich set of symbolic values. Light is perfectly pure, having no taint of its own, yet makes it possible to see all imperfections. Light clarifies everything, and nothing can obstruct the buddha's own light. Light that streams forth from a buddha does not merely illuminate the people it touches. Contact with that light also transforms those people. Thus, the *Splendid Vision* describes the liberative effect of Shakyamuni's samadhi-generated light: the blind see, the deaf hear, and, in general, every being's hopes are realized in full. As Gómez writes, they "share in the meditator's experience," the buddha's own experience of enlightened peace.

The brilliance that shoots forth from Shakyamuni, illuminating the whole universe, is the vivid materialization of his samadhi. It is an *apocalypse*, uncovering that which had hitherto been hidden. What is revealed? The fact that, despite all appearances, our cosmos really is a paradise free from want and suffering, where even wraiths, demons, and ogres are radiant with benevolence. Despite all appearances, we are enlightened. To the extent that Shulkshina and Shulivujna accept this samadhi's revelation as reality, capital *R*, the *Splendid Vision* participates in the second dimension of scripturality (truth). For their communities of interest, scriptures are worlds unto themselves that disclose the spatiotemporal nexus of the cosmos in its most elemental form. In order to see this splendid vision, however, one must have the eyes to see. Early Protestants considered those eyes to be a gift of the holy spirit, graced only to a select few; everybody else be damned. Shakyamuni's transforming light, by contrast, touches all creatures, great and small. All are enlightened. All are given the splendid vision needed to see the *Splendid Vision*. To read the sutra as scripture is to reconvene the great assembly on Potalaka Mountain again and again and again.

Authority: From India to Rome and Back Again

PRESENTISM REVISITED

For the professional historian, *presentism* is a dirty word. Commonly, this term is used to deprecate historical analyses that judge past events and people by present-day standards. Thus, for instance, when a student in my introduction to Buddhism class asks (as one always does), if the buddha was so enlightened, why was he such a sexist? I might respond, that is a presentist question, demonstrating little sensitivity to the historical context in which Shakyamuni lived or the gender norms dominant at that time and place. I might then give a mini-lecture on the history of Buddhist disciplinary rules, explaining that the early community was deeply conservative on social matters and that many rules of monastic behavior seem to have been instituted with the express purpose of avoiding public gossip or scandal, and not toward any overtly "spiritual" aim.

Nevertheless, despite presentism's potential for distorting the past, presentist questions can also lead to clarity by calling attention to obvious truths hidden in plain sight. Often, they serve as "emperor's new clothes" questions, saying that which otherwise might go without saying. And thus a second answer to the query about Shakyamuni's sexism may be: if you really think that an enlightened being cannot be sexist, then Shakyamuni was probably not enlightened. And that answer might, in turn, lead to a second minilecture in which I explain that *enlightenment* is not a state of being but a value judgment; its rhetorical purpose is to mark specific values that a speaker considers to be intrinsically good or wise as also being universally beneficial, honorable, and true. This second lecture might conclude, in turn, that anybody who proposes that Shakyamuni was enlightened but not committed to sexual equality is also implicitly asserting that equality between the sexes is not a universal good. The two minilectures are completely different, and I am hard-pressed to say which one is more salient. In sum, presentist questions and presentist categories can be especially powerful tools insofar as they do not neatly fit the facts; insofar as they ring with the dissonance of a historical tin ear; insofar as they complicate that which might otherwise appear straightforward; insofar as they are incapable of piety. The space opened up by the disjuncture between current interests and past contexts must bring the rough edges of both into greater relief.

So it is that scripture and myth, as modern categories with no exact parallels in Sanskrit, open our eyes to the *Splendid Vision* and reveal dimensions of the sutra that would have been invisible to Shulkshina or Shulivujna, or the dharma preachers they were exhorted to revere. Thus far, this essay has sought to frame the sutra's opening passages in contemporary terms. Now, as we move deeper into the text, let us also recognize that the interpretive process works in both directions. Not only does the past change to meet the present gaze but also our native intellectual categories are themselves modified and refined through their encounter with the past.

This process of recursive change is true for our primary category, scripture. Although I defined this genre in terms of three distinct elements, we have witnessed that when those analytic elements are brought to bear on an actual text they do not remain distinct. The three—value, truth, and existential meaning—overlap, twine into each other, and at times may even become indistinguishable. Practically, this means that we cannot simply apply the three dimensions point by point: first examining the essential value the *Splendid Vision* held for Shulkshina and Shulivujna; then considering the sutra as a source of essential truths; finally, investigating how Shulkshina and Shulivujna brought those teachings into their lives. Such an approach is distractingly tidy. Applied with mechanical efficiency, this formula will kill the text, when our desire is to feel how it lives.

So now let us shift course. Rather than inquiring into the formal, generic elements of scripture, let us instead wonder about people who accept scriptural texts in their lives, asking emperor's new clothing questions: Why do people want special texts? Why do people want to know occult truths? Why might people willingly disregard their own experiences in order to accept texts as authoritative? Why do people change their behavior on the say-so of a book? These questions can be addressed through two words: authority and power. The complex intersection of scriptural elements nos. 1 and 2—essential value and essential truth—can be reframed thus: scriptures are sources of authority. The present section considers the nature of scriptural authority. The complex intersection of scriptural elements nos. 2 and 3—essential truth and essential action—can be reframed thus: scriptures are sources of power. The next major section of the essay considers the nature of scriptural power. After that is the conclusion.

I WANT TO SAY ONE WORD TO YOU. JUST ONE WORD.

Years ago I lived in India, in a small town named Fardapur, while researching Buddhist history at the nearby Ajanta Caves. Naturally I made several friends among the locals. Although we passed odd hours laughing and joking about many subjects without restraint, there was one question I wanted to ask but never did. It was a question about wealth, or rather the perception of wealth. The gap between my friends and myself was enormous. At the time, a plane ticket cost over $1,000 and my research stipend was princely, while they sometimes earned only $1 or $2 a day. How presumptuous it would have been for me to interrogate R. or T. about the degree to which his experience of his own poverty was exacerbated by my presence in his life. Certainly this was something they thought about as well. The topic was even discussed around the edges. But I wonder how much they gossiped about the imbalance between my prosperity and their lack of it. Did my material well-being diminish their psychic well-being? They knew they were poor. But how much was their experience of impoverishment aggravated by the fact that a man possessing, what was to them, unattainable wealth talked, ate, and laughed with them every day? To put the matter crassly: were they poor and happy, or poor but happy? Or were they wretched?

The *Splendid Vision* has no such compunction about raising the subject of personal pain. On page after page the sutra recites a litany of the ways in which people suffer. They are blind, deaf, poor, diseased, crazy, full of aches and pains. They are afflicted by acne or, worse, leprosy. They die young. They are immoral, jealous, frivolous, and greedy. They are stupid. They misunderstand the truth right in front of their faces. Ghosts and demons attack them and their loved ones. They constantly dream about their own deaths. Human beings have so many reasons to be anxious. Yet even though "they see each other being laid out on biers ready for the charnel ground, they do not conceive meritorious thoughts or unwavering faith. So after death, they suffer misery again and again" (§49).

The *Splendid Vision*'s comprehensive register of samsara's failings is hardly unique to this sutra. The teaching of Buddhist doctrine often begins with the four noble truths, the first of which is a one-word Sanskrit exclamation: *duhkha*. This word is usually translated as suffering, but there is more to it than that. Its etymological components, *duh* and *kha*, translate as "bad" and "space," metaphoric for a range of existential maladies. To experience *duhkha* is to experience oneself as being in the wrong world, in a bad space—physically, mentally, emotionally—filled with suffering, unsatisfactoriness, dis-ease, unacceptability, imperfection. As a foundational teaching, *duhkha* reduces life's panorama to a single, readily comprehensible, easily repeatable, and seemingly irrefutable shibboleth. In the words of Shakyamuni's first sermon:

> Birth is *duhkha*. Old age is *duhkha*. Disease is *duhkha*. Death is *duhkha*. Separation from the pleasant is *duhkha*. Contact with the unpleasant is *duhkha*. Not getting what you want, though you strive after it: that too is *duhkha*.[37]

As soon as one is looking for *duhkha*, what cannot be perceived as *duhkha*?

Perhaps Shulkshina and Shulivujna were deeply familiar with the ever-likely misfortunes of worldly existence. For while the *Splendid Vision* claims that, long ago, light shot out from Shakyamuni, filling billions of worlds, revealing the buddha's glory, power, and compassion, and while the *Splendid Vision* informs Shulkshina and Shulivujna that they themselves were present at this event (as were you, dear reader), the *Splendid Vision* also reminds Shulkshina and Shulivujna that the world in which they now live is a place filled with deaf, blind, sick, and suffering fools. In order to promote the hope that our universe may become one in which compassion reigns supreme, all beings joined in love and harmony, the *Splendid Vision* must constantly, again and again, reiterate the many ways in which the world presently falls short. A person must acknowledge the disease before she will seek the cure—the cure being nothing other than the *Splendid Vision* itself.

As soon as one is looking for *duhkha*, what in this world cannot be perceived as *duhkha*? But one must be looking! Indeed, the stories told of Shakyamuni's youth suggest that however ubiquitous *duhkha* "really" is, he remained unaware of its reality until the age of twenty-nine. Prince Siddhartha considered himself happy—*sukha*, literally, in a good place—until he learned better. Does one suffer if one does not learn to perceive one's experiences as suffering? Might the noble truth of *duhkha* be as much a matter of scriptural myth as it is one of existential math? For does not the acceptance of *duhkha* as a foundational truth divide the Buddhist from the non-Buddhist? How difficult would it be for a committed Buddhist to acknowledge that there may be individuals who do not perceive *duhkha* as a self-evident truth about our world and yet who live joyful and fulfilling lives?

Though this last fanciful imagining may seem tangential to the analysis of *Splendid Vision* as scripture, in fact it cuts right to the heart of the matter. For although we have analyzed scripturality in terms of three dimensions—a text is a scripture insofar as it is accepted as a source of universal value, ultimate reality, and meaningful action—we might also compact all this verbiage into a single word: authority. Scripture is a literature of (religious) authority. The *Splendid Vision* is an authoritative text. Those who recognize the authority of this or other Buddhist scriptures find themselves able to see *duhkha* and the causes of *duhkha* wherever they look. Those who do not recognize the sutra's authority may have scant reason to look for *duhkha* in the first place.

THE AUTHORITY EFFECT

Authority is foundational. It is the logical ground of scripturality. So let us now consider authority directly. Just as we turned to sixteenth-century Europe to understand the category *scripture*, so our hybrid Indian/Western, modern/ancient reading of the *Splendid Vision* must transport us elsewhere. In this case, let us travel to the rolling hills of ancient Rome. The word *authority* comes into English from Latin *auctoritas*, and the manner in which Romans used this term clarifies our contemporary usage.

One way to specify the meaning of an abstract category is by distinguishing it from other categories to which it is closely related. In classical Rome, as today, authority was associated with, but differentiated from, power. Let me explain through an example.[38] In the most ancient period of Roman history, before the Empire and before the Republic, Rome was a monarchy ruled by kings (eighth to sixth centuries B.C.E.). Royal succession, however, was not hereditary or dynastic. That is, Rome's throne was not passed down automatically from a monarch to his son. Rather, kingship in Rome was an elected position, voted upon by citizens who would become the king's subjects.

The electoral process had two steps. First, the body of Roman citizens exercised *power,* by selecting one individual to be the ruler and acclaiming him for that position. Second, the Roman Senate—an institution composed of patriarchs from Rome's most venerable and wealthy families—*authorized* the people's choice.

The mass of citizens had the power to choose. Indeed, the Latin word for power, *potestas,* is derived from a verb, *posse,* "to be able." However, the senatorial elite did not trust the people. How could senators be certain that the masses would select the right man to lead them? After all, patricians and plebeians have different, if not conflicting, political agendas and social needs. Thus, the Roman electoral process had a second step. To assume the robes and office of monarch, a candidate also required authorization from the Senate. Authority, *auctoritas* in Latin, is derived from the verb *augere,* literally, to increase, augment, or complete. The Senate's authority augmented and finalized the people's power. It elevated the status of a decision from being debatable to being legitimate and correct. It raised a man to the status of king. Without the confirmation of authority, the exercise of power was incomplete. Authority is crucial because, in the long run, might alone does not make right.

For Rome, authority was a quality distinct from power. It was held by the few, not the many. Authority did not accomplish its aims through any form of coercive action. If a group of people saw themselves as having been wronged, they could try to argue their grievances verbally, editorializing or speechifying, and if such nonviolent tactics failed, the people had the ability to then rampage and riot. Categorically, direct action taken to change another's mind or behavior is the expression of power, not authority. Authority, rather, is a quality of social hierarchies, wherein a person who is structurally superior is perceived as justified in his actions precisely because he is superior. One notorious example from U.S. history is former president Richard Nixon's assertion that "When the president does it that means that it is not illegal."[39] In other words, for Nixon, a president's actions are necessarily legitimate and legal merely by virtue of his structural position as the head of government. Likewise, we find this theory of authority tacit in Jean Calvin's claim, "God's will is so much the highest rule of righteousness that whatever he wills, by the very fact that he wills it, must be considered righteous."[40] Just as Nixon expected the American populace to acquiesce to his actions merely because he was president, and just as Calvin expected humanity to accept god's judgments merely because god is god, so relations of authority in general require inferiors to express respect, faith, obedience, trust, and acceptance for the words/actions of that person (or group) who is structurally superior. The inferior accepts the superior for no reason other than the superior is above him: this *otherness* is the key to authority. Authority necessarily marks hierarchy and inequality. Ready participation in relations of authority marks an acceptance that all human beings are not equal in all ways.

The historian of religions Bruce Lincoln has suggested that, from a contemporary analytic perspective, authority should be understood as an "effect," emergent from hierarchical social relationships. Lincoln explains,

> I take the [authority] effect to be the result of the conjuncture of the right speaker, the right speech and delivery, the right staging and props, the right time and place, and an audience whose historically and culturally conditioned expectations establish the parameters of what is judged "right" in all these instances. When these crucial givens of the discursive situation combine in such a way as to produce attitudes of trust, respect, docility, acceptance, even reverence, in the audience . . . "authority" is the result.[41]

The staging of the *Splendid Vision*'s opening scene is composed to produce just such an "authority effect." It does so at two levels. Within the narrative, the elite nature of Shakyamuni's audience, his entrance into a samadhi, his illumination of the entire universe with brilliant light, signaling both the vast extent of his sovereignty and the compassionate characteristic of that sovereignty, all culminate in Manjushri's prediction:

> I see a large congregation of bodhisattvas and recognize the omen of a
> grand assembly.... I see many hundreds of thousands of millions of bodhi-
> sattvas who have heard prophecies of their own future buddhahood and
> recognize the omen of a momentous discourse on dharma: a discourse that
> will fulfill the hopes of many hundreds of thousands of millions of beings,
> who will gain great knowledge. (§12)

This first level of authorization then opens up into a second: the level
at which the *Splendid Vision*'s audience members grant the sutra authority over themselves. Manjushri's prediction completes the scene,
informing Shulkshina and Shulivujna, in effect, that Shakyamuni possesses authority because he deserves authority: the buddha's presence augments—legitimates and completes—the cosmos. Implicitly,
the sutra is also teaching that the cosmos sans Shakyamuni would be
a locus of unrelieved *duhkha*. So given the buddha's compassionate
presence, those who faithfully accept his authority are guaranteed to
attain an equal position of authority themselves. Indeed, even those
who do not acknowledge it right now will awaken someday to recognize the darkness that blinded their eyes to the truth. With this last
claim, the process of authorization is occluded: Shakyamuni's authority is represented, not as an "effect" but rather as an inescapable en-
tanglement of the cosmos itself.

   The *Splendid Vision* does not manufacture this authority effect
only through its detailed, hierarchical representation of characters
and events. The sutra's literary form also contributes to that effect.
The word *author* is related to authority, and we have noted several
ways in which the *Splendid Vision* participates in a general Buddhist
anxiety regarding the authorship of sutras. If the *Splendid Vision* did
not begin "Thus have I heard," or conclude with Ananda's pledge to remember and preserve it for posterity, it would remain an anonymous
text. As such, the *Splendid Vision* would not be authorized as a sutra,
for it would lack the authority of Shakyamuni's original authorship.
The appropriation and repetition of the formal aspects of the sutra

genre augments trust in the *Splendid Vision*'s content: the doctrines it teaches, the practices it advises, and the cult figures it extols.

This beginning and ending are, in turn, augmented by the imprimatur of tradition. Recall the introduction's earlier example of Marcel Duchamp's 1917 sculpture *Fountain*, a urinal that he submitted under the name Richard Mutt for inclusion in an exhibit staged by the Society of Independent Artists. New York's artists detested *Fountain* when it was submitted for exhibition, in part because Duchamp appropriated and repeated the formal aspects of the fine art genre—he signed and dated the urinal—in order to recontextualize and legitimate an object they perceived as vulgar and inappropriate. Similarly, were the *Splendid Vision* to use all the generic markers of a sutra in order to present a radically atypical dharma—for example encouraging the worship of rival deities like Vishnu and Shiva, or expressing contempt for the four noble truths—one might doubt that its authorizing effects would have met with such success. But the *Splendid Vision* is quite clear in its promise: even if you kill your own mother and father, the sutra will save you from hellfire, unless you are an unbeliever, skeptical about the buddha's dharma (§§76, 92). There is nothing unconventional about that.

To cite Bruce Lincoln one more time: "Religious claims are the means by which certain objects, places, speakers, and speech-acts are invested with an authority, the source of which lies *outside the human*."[42] On these terms, the *Splendid Vision* may be called a perfect religious text. For this sutra both proclaims the existence of a perfect extrahuman authority and uses multiple literary devices and strategies to identify itself as embodying that authority.

THE SOCIAL PSYCHOLOGY OF AUTHORITY

Why is the establishment of authority so important? One reason is, simply, that Shulkshina and Shulivujna were born more than one millennium after Shakyamuni's death. For them to take the *Splendid Vision* as valuable and true directives for life, the sutra's words had to be augmented with a grand drama that itself made sense within the natural history of Buddhist traditions. This sutra's introduction and conclusion do not mark the *Splendid Vision* as a unique sutra. Rather they show it to be a typical sutra, though it proclaims itself to be the greatest sutra of them all.

A second reason is less obvious, but also more interesting, not least because it harks back to the "cool factor." Recall, the cool factor served to introduce the difficulty of apprehending the link between the subjective and the objective, experience and action. My student tattooed herself बोधिसत्त्व. But what did her justification, "It's cool," mean? Was she saying, "My friends will like me better because of this tattoo," or "I think Devanagari script is pretty," or "These letters remind me to be a better person," or was she saying, simply, "It's cool"? To my ears, the student's explanation was no explanation. I could not restate her motivation in words that made sense to me but also respected her personal integrity.

Earlier, I used this anecdote to introduce a seminal problem for scholars of the humanities. Namely, scholars look for a determinate relation among intention, meaning, and value. To find the significance of an action we look at the conscious intentions that motivate the action. This mode of operation, in turn, presupposes an anthropological model in which human beings are capable of self-knowledge as well as self-determination. When these capabilities are idealized, we speak of *enlightenment*. Enlightened people hold deep insight into their own minds and act upon this self-knowledge with radical autonomy. In Western philosophy, this position was most fully articulated in the writings of Immanuel Kant, the culminating figure of Europe's eighteenth-century Age of Enlightenment. For Kant, the human mind, in its essential nature, is free from the controlling influence of forces outside its own conscious will; each of us possesses a will more powerful than any internal instinct, emotion, desire, or biological process, let alone forces of external coercion. And thus Kant held that we have the capacity to formulate perfectly rational principles of behavior, as well as the obligation to adhere to those rational principles without the slightest deviation.[43] In this Enlightenment ideal, in other words, each of us is capable of serving as her own personal authority, complete in herself.

Yet—and here's the problem—contemporary neurobiological research has given the lie to this ideal. Technological advances unimaginable fifty years ago, let alone two thousand, reveal that members of the species *Homo sapiens* are physically and psychically incapable of enlightened autonomy. There is an active debate as to whether free will is real or an illusion. Do the volitions that we experience subjectively in our minds really cause the actions we perform out in the world? Or is the link between will and action an illusion produced milliseconds after the fact, a retrospective representation of cognitive processes that are unconscious and indeterminate?[44] The debate rages. Still, even as psychologists and neurobiologists disagree about the philosophical limits of free will, they concur that sociality is built into human biology at the neural level. Our brains do not function properly unless they come into contact, emotionally and psychically, with other brains. As one recent study puts it, "The human brain is a social organ."[45] Another observes, "Investigations into the physiology of relatedness now tell us that attachment penetrates to the neural core of what it means to be a human being."[46] We are starting to learn that the architecture of the brain invalidates any anthropological theory that represents human beings as transcendentally free, fully autonomous, or capable of thoroughgoing emotional detachment. It is possible that biological science may soon do to the belief in enlightened autonomy what astronomy once did to the belief that the sun revolves around the earth.

Indeed, I must guess (since I cannot know) that anybody reading these words recognizes this situation for himself or herself. You do not need anecdotes about tattoos, and you do not need fMRI studies, to observe your own personal degree of self-determination. No matter whether you revere Shakyamuni as an awakened buddha, or revere Jesus as the son of god, or Krishna as Vishnu's avatara, or Muhammad as the Seal of the Prophets, or whether you have no strong ideological commitments, or are a Wiccan, a Gaian, or an ecoanarchist, or take reason as sufficient unto itself, you know for yourself whether, right here and now, your thoughts, reactions, body, and life are fully under your own conscious control. My guess? They are not. My guess? Whatever your personal ideal for self-knowledge and conscious action, your lived reality falls short.

Why, then, is the establishment of authority so important? Because even though we are incapable of full self-authorization, even though we cannot fulfill the buddha's command to be islands unto ourselves, we nevertheless do require a sense of certainty and psychic closure. Without our having recourse to authority in some form, the indeterminacies of naked existence would become overwhelming. In the words of neurologist Robert Burton,

> Without a circuit breaker, indecision and inaction would rule the day. What is needed is a mental switch that stops infinite ruminations and calms our fears of missing an unknown superior alternative.... The feeling of knowing is a marvelous adaptation that solves a very real metaphysical dilemma of how to reach a conclusion.[47]

When Burton's "feeling of knowing" becomes a feeling of certainty, conviction, and rightness, we might speak of authority. Authority is the objectification of this subjective need. Authority augments and completes. In this regard, it is also worth noting that under Roman legal theory, an individual could not wield *auctoritas* unless he was also judged a member of the *prudentes*, the community of the learned.

A recent book by Paul Bloom, a research psychologist at Yale, takes Burton's point one step further. Bloom explores the oddities of pleasure and perversity. Why do some people take pleasure from cannibalism? Why will someone pay millions for a signed masterpiece but next to nothing for a near-perfect forgery? Why was Duchamp's *Fountain* so displeasing to his contemporaries? Bloom proposes that in all cases, pleasure is a function of an "essentialist intuition."[48] Citing John Locke's definition of essence as "the very being of anything, whereby it is what it is," Bloom avers that, as human beings, we are hardwired to experience positive feelings—*sukha*—when we somehow feel that we have grasped an essence, and thereby experienced something real in its integrity.[49] If indeed there is a fundamental human need for making "sense of reality" in terms of determinate essences, then pleasure is impossible without authority.[50] For in these terms, authority is nothing other than the determination of determinacy. Though Bloom cannot know how close his theory comes to the teachings of the *Splendid Vision*, they concur: without authority, all is *duhkha*, suffering.

In Rome, the Senate's authority finalized the people's power. The social structure expressed a perceived need for a small elite to circumscribe the masses. At a personal level, as well, each of us relies upon something beyond ourselves to serve as a touchstone of legitimacy and closure. All of us—even the coolest बोधिसत्त्व—participate in relations of authority. An authority might be a superhuman entity like the buddha and Jesus. Or it might be a concept like love, rationality, or enlightenment. Or it might be another human being like a financial adviser or police officer. Or it might be a Mahayana sutra. Possibilities for the specific location of authority shift with circumstances, nations, eras, languages, genders, and every other factor imaginable. What does not shift, however, is the human need to feel that, in a given circumstance, one has acted correctly, or understood correctly, or made the wise choice. Like all living scriptures, the *Splendid Vision* speaks directly to this need.

The Play of Power

PLEASURE TO THE PEOPLE!

There is a nice irony in Paul Bloom's proposition that our pleasures are structured by our genetic need to experience essences. For, if Buddhism is commonly associated with one philosophical debate, it is the debate over essentialism, with Shakyamuni at the vanguard of the antiessentialist camp. According to early Buddhism, Siddhartha awakened as a buddha when he fully saw and recognized the implications of "no-self," the understanding that human beings have no permanent essence. Now in middle age, I consider myself the same person I was when a student and youth, and until the moment of death I expect to feel myself the same person still. But for Buddhism I am just a figment of my imagination. This inner sense of continuous and substantial identity is really my misapprehension of a process in flux. Further, the Mahayana theorization of "emptiness" expanded early Buddhism's antiessentialism beyond personal identity to include objects, ideas, and indeed all conceivable phenomena. For an enlightened buddha, every "essence" is devoid of essence. So, if the truth of emptiness means that there are no essences to enjoy in enlightenment, then it would seem that enlightenment is the death of pleasure.

First impressions, in this case, are deceptive. Canonical descriptions of Shakyamuni meditating on the night of his enlightenment describe him as pursuing essences. Beneath the bodhi tree, he expanded his mind and examined the diverse thoughts flowing through it, recognizing and categorizing the nuanced particularity of each mental moment. Earlier we read John Locke's definition of essence: that by which a particular phenomenon "is what it is." The *Mulasarvastivada vinaya* (another text buried at Gilgit that we also encountered earlier in this essay) uses the self-same phrase to describe the interior reasoning by which Shakyamuni gained enlightenment. To cite a line: "He recognized the noble truth of *duhkha* for what it is, 'the noble truth of *duhkha*.' He recognized the noble truth of the arising of *duhkha* for what it is, 'the arising of *duhkha*.'"[51] Again and again the text repeats, Shakyamuni "recognized x for what it is," where x represents every possible cognitive state. Even in Mahayana Buddhism, Shakyamuni's profound insight is described as knowledge of *thusness*, ultimate reality seen ultimately, in its essence. Thus, returning to Bloom's pleasure thesis, perhaps nobody has more pleasure than an enlightened buddha, for enlightenment is found in the delectation of the innermost essence of that which is most essential.

In this light, I invite you to return to the translation for a moment, to reread section §44, where Shakyamuni explains the title *the splen-*

did vision in which one observes living beings and reveals buddhafields through the empowerment of all tathagatas, which is both the name of the sutra and a samadhi. Section §44 draws a straight line from enlightenment to pleasure. Buddhas empower bodhisattvas to attain states of deep concentration within which they are able to read others' minds. This parapsychological skill, in turn, enables bodhisattvas to directly observe karmic cause and effect. With eyes unimpeded by past, future, distance, or solid matter, bodhisattvas see that people who accept the buddhas' authority enjoy fulfilling lives, while those who reject the buddhas' authority suffer. Knowing this, bodhisattvas are spurred to action. Their compassionate engagement with the faithless has two steps. First, bodhisattvas use their powers to satisfy worldly desires. Second, they teach the dharma. The new converts, in turn, gain spiritual merit. And the force of that spiritual merit catapults the converts—now also bodhisattvas—into heavenly buddhafields. In these buddhafields, the new bodhisattvas meet more buddhas and continue their spiritual training until, ultimately, they become buddhas themselves. Now enlightened, those former evildoers serve as sources of authority and power for new bodhisattvas.

In Paul Bloom's terms, beings who follow the *Splendid Vision* renounce worthless pleasures, born of a mania for sham essences, in favor of transcendent pleasures, born of engagement with essential reality. From beginning to end, the sutra implies that the cosmos, sans Shakyamuni, would be a place of unrelieved suffering. But this sutra is nothing if not self-congratulatory. For of course Shakyamuni's essence remains ever present—glory be to the *Splendid Vision*!—empowering Shulkshina and Shulivujna to bring ever more pleasure, joy, happiness, and enchantment into their lives.

And with only slightly less tenacity than the sutra, this interpretive essay has repeated: The label *scripture* does not pertain to specific texts per se; nor is scripturality an innate property of tangible objects. Scripturality arises, rather, when individuals or communities transact their identities through texts. Scriptural relationships are intangible and fluid relationships that give rise to material consequences. They are relationships that change the world. Yes, Luther and Calvin would demand that the Bible is god's self-revelation and thus essentially holy. And yes, Shulkshina and Shulivujna might acquiesce to the *Splendid Vision*'s claim that it is the buddha-dharma and thus essentially true. For us, however, the Bible and *Splendid Vision* are scriptures, not because they reveal divinity, but because people like Luther and Calvin, Shulkshina and Shulivujna, treat these texts' words as divine authority made manifest. The previous section explored the nature of religious authority in relation to the *Splendid Vision*. Still, although scriptures are authoritative texts, that is not all they are. Our model of scripturality places power after authority.

Scriptures participate in relationships of power. To say that we find *scripture* where we find a text that a community expects to be performed, not just read or heard (scripturality element no. 3), is to say that scriptural "power" is revealed in bodily performance: how members of a scripture's community live the text in time. Let us now turn to a fuller consideration of the *Splendid Vision* as a source of power and pleasure, two values inextricable from the matter of performance. For we can only really speak of a text as *scripture* when, after having been accepted as a source of authority, value, and truth (scriptural elements nos. 1 and 2), the book lives, as it were, beyond the book.

EMBODIED PERFORMANCE

Buddhism is a religion of performance. By playing the part, one becomes what one might be. Just consider the *Splendid Vision*'s section 44. From beginning to end, the process is performative. The first act, though it happens offstage, entails the bodhisattva's full acceptance of the tathagatas' authority: an act of faith that transforms the bodhisattva into a telepath. It must be a curious thrill to read others' minds. But the bodhisattva does not practice her new art with canned objectivity, like a mystical market researcher. Every sour thought she reads is a spur to action. She gives of herself again and again, becoming a bodhisattva by enacting the deeds of a bodhisattva: satisfying others with gifts of what they want as well as what they need. The acceptance of a gift has no less transformative force than giving one. By interacting with a bodhisattva, people who once did wrong now do right. They too play the bodhisattva's part: first by placing faith in the tathagatas, then by giving others what they want and need. And because pleasure is never far from power, if bodhisattvas so desire, they can act out the grand drama of Buddhist authority and power while luxuriating in paradisiacal buddhafields—happy ending, guaranteed.

Section 44 can be read as the script of an ideal existence. Likewise, the rituals described by Shakyamuni, Vajrapani, Avalokiteshvara, and the three yakshinis are scripted for a happy ending. But when we think about scripture as performative, we should not, in fact, look to the formal protocols of drama. Why? Dramatic acting, as we normally experience it in the theater, or while watching TV or a movie, is a practice of symbolic embodiment. There are three parties to this dramatic transaction: author, actor, and audience. The author composes his insights and emotions on the page; the actors embody the dramatis personae of the script; the audience sits and watches. Actors serve as bodies: corporeal intermediaries that transmit the author's symbolic values to the minds of his audience's members. There is an odd slippage here, for the actor's body, as the medium of transmission, is crucial to the overall process (otherwise, members of the audience could just sit down and read the script), yet the actor's body is also devalued on its own account. To paraphrase performance theorist Erika Fischer-Lichte, dramatic embodiment as a symbolic process strips the actor's body of its corporeality and forces it to "undergo a process of disembodiment."[52] We laud actors (like Meryl Streep at her best) who strip away their own personal modes of dressing, walking, speaking, gesturing, and so on in order that they might employ their bodies fully in the realization of their dramatic characters as scripted; we mock actors (like Keanu Reeves) who play every role with the self-same affect. In Hollywood and on Broadway, the best actors separate their dramatic roles from their lives. They put on a spectacle of otherness and astound us with their skill at representing that which they are not.

Scriptural performance is not like this. Embodiment is key to scriptural performance too, but it is not *symbolic* embodiment. Embodied performance does not even require a written script. If we think about the bodhisattva of section 44 as performing the *Splendid Vision*, we would not reckon her as using her body to transmit symbolic values from the *Splendid Vision*'s dharma preacher to the sutra's audience. Rather, scriptural embodiment entails the fusing of body and mind. Normally intangible drives, emotions, philosophies, and ideals become concretized through gestures of the body, and the body, in turn, becomes abstracted as a form of mind. The bodhisattva who observes living beings and leads them to buddhafields does not "mean" or "represent" anything by acting thus: she does what she is and she is what she does.

In a nice coincidence, Jerzy Grotowski, a theorist whose mid-1960s writings on theater remain influential to this day, described figures like our section 44 bodhisattva as "holy actors." Grotowski was writing about performance in the secular theater. Still, he chose this religious metaphor because, in his view, holy actors do not separate their lives from their art. A holy actor approaches his performance with an "attitude of giving and receiving which springs from true love: in other words, self-sacrifice."[53] Indeed, to the degree that a performance embodies this love, the actor needs nothing more than his own body in order to realize his part. He needs no props, costumes, scenery, stage, makeup, lighting, sound effects, not even spectators. Thus Grotowski called his theater the "poor theater." Everything superfluous, everything that might draw attention from the actor's expressive self, might be stripped away.[54] For the fewer props an actor possesses the more he is required, in Grotowski's words, to "make a total gift of himself."[55]

This brings us back to Paul Bloom's theory connecting essences and pleasures. What is a total gift but the giving of one's essence? And who could receive such a gift and not respond? Who could encounter a human being in his raw humanity but remain unmoved? At its best, contemporary performance art erases the line between performer and audience. It plays upon audience members' sense of responsibility—their ability to respond—to inspire countergifts of equal intensity, and ideally equal love. To receive pleasure without needing to give pleasure in return is to be emotionally undead.

It is this play between gift and countergift that is at the heart of scripture as a source of existential power. Scripture is not a literature of spectatorship; it is a literature of responsibility. The *Splendid Vision* requires its audience's total participation. When Shakyamuni tells the bodhisattva Manjushri,

> Son of good family, if somebody has not planted any roots of virtue, or has not seen a tathagata, or has not received a prophecy of future buddhahood, then he will fail to hear this dharma discourse (§50),

he is telling Shulkshina and Shulivujna that this is their drama, their deep reality. Whatever awful and tawdry details fritter away their days, their roots of merit are secure; they have seen the tathagata; their future buddhahood is prophesied and guaranteed. The same holds true, of course, for you. All that is needed is that you respond by accepting the gifts of power the sutra offers: worshiping deities the *Splendid Vision* presents for worship, reciting the incantations the *Splendid Vision* presents for recitation, and living the life of the bodhisattva. And if you are unable to follow its directives? The sutra has a response:

> Unless someone is empowered by the tathagata, he cannot hear this dharma discourse, or remember it, or worship it, or write it, or have it written, or place his faith in it. Even if he comes into contact with this dharma discourse, he won't hear it. Or if he hears it, his mind will be distracted as he listens. He will not show it faith or honor. (§65)[56]

You are empowered by the tathagata only if you take the power he offers and embody it. To take this to heart is to treat the *Splendid Vision* as scripture.

ON YAKSHINIS

Is this why my student tattooed बोधिसत्त्व on her left shoulder? Perhaps Grotowski's vision of the holy actor inspired her to respond to the sutra through body modification. Maybe she just took Erika Fischer-Lichte's discussion of embodied performance literally, word for word: "The character exists in the actor's physical performance alone and is brought forth both by his performative acts and his particular corporeality."[57] To the best of my knowledge, there is no active cult to Shankhini, or any yakshini, on the University of California, San Diego campus. But even without such a community, she might have been expecting that her embodied performance would win the yakshini's blessing. A lifelong tattoo seems a small price to pay for lifelong fame, fabulousness, wealth, power, and health.

Shankhini's direction to place her incantation on one's body is only one among the *Splendid Vision*'s many descriptions of embodied practices, all of which are means for a person to harness the transformative power contained in the sutra and its incantations. As we move toward a conclusion, let us shift attention to these yakshinis—Shankhini, Anopama, and Bhima. For me, at least, the yakshinis are the sutra's most interesting characters. Miranda Shaw's study of Buddhist goddesses in India calls yakshinis "voluptuous, magical nature spirits."[58] This is true, so far as it goes, though yakshinis generally receive more prosaic characterizations such as female semidivine spirits, or demonesses. In the *Splendid Vision*, yakshinis are also highly accomplished bodhisattvas. In the oscillation between their earthy, sometimes malignant, animal nature and their spiritual glory, yakshinis serve as idealized models for the *Splendid Vision*'s human audience. The *Splendid Vision*'s yakshinis are transformed beings. We can only hope to improve ourselves with such success.

Indeed, it was the *Splendid Vision*'s yakshinis that first brought the sutra to my attention. When I was a graduate student my principal research focused on Ajanta, a Buddhist monastery in India dating to the fifth century renowned for its paintings and sculptures. My intention was to use Ajanta's art to reconstruct the day-to-day nature of Buddhism in ancient India. But during a trip to Ajanta I was surprised to see that so much of the monastery's iconography featured yakshinis. The scholarship I read in preparation for the visit was far more interested in doctrines than in people, and it had little information about these figures. The few mentions of yakshinis I read did not place them in an ideologically Buddhist context or treat them as Buddhist divinities. Yet, at Ajanta, the local community's regard for yakshinis was unmistakable. Yakshinis seemed to be everywhere, in paintings and sculptures and shrines, in nearly every structure at the site. Because yakshinis play such a central role in the *Splendid Vision*, I began to study this sutra, hoping that it would illuminate the Buddhist mentality evidenced at Ajanta.

Three yakshinis—Anopama, Shankhini, and Bhima—are pivotal in the *Splendid Vision*'s second half. So what is a yakshini? Generally speaking, yakshinis are earthbound divinities, usually associated with a particular locale. It has been said that every village in India has its own goddess, or yakshini, living under a nearby field, or inside a large tree at the village's edge, in the jungle, and so on. Spirits of this sort are often characterized as "ambivalent," since they can be both beneficent and maleficent. That is to say, satisfied yakshinis have the power to make women fertile, to make harvests abundant, or to protect villages from pestilence and banditry. When angered, however, yakshinis develop a ferocious appetite, which they satisfy by eating little children and destroying lives. Yakshinis are the very disease and pestilence they protect others against. In this dual role, yakshinis are probably the most common and most prevalent form of superhuman entity in India, from ancient days until the present.

I would suggest that the yakshinis' popularity is a direct function of their all-too-human nature. Who among your loving friends does not, at times, reveal an inner demon, or, when provoked, flail about like a bloodthirsty monster? Wrath and rage are our inheritance as animal beings, which, with greater or lesser ease and success, we keep under control. It is a truism within the academic study of religion that divinities are the objectified expressions of human values. We study gods and goddesses, angels, vampires, and yakshinis in order to understand what people love and loathe about themselves. And thus in the case of Shankhini, Anopama, and Bhima, we can consider these yakshinis, their stories, their actions, and their promises, in order to grasp how the *Splendid Vision*'s author and audience might have understood the sutra's power to domesticate and transform—a psychic makeover, from monster to bodhisattva to buddha, in three easy steps.

In the *Splendid Vision*, Anopama, Shankhini, and Bhima seem to be anything but wild. The sutra calls them accomplished bodhisattvas and great goddesses. Despite this esteem, however, the sutra is still careful to distinguish yakshinis as a class from the buddha and, more especially, from celestial bodhisattvas like Avalokiteshvara and Manjushri. To differentiate the three groups, we might characterize buddhas and celestial bodhisattvas as "natural" insiders, while yakshinis would be "naturalized" insiders. That is, buddhas and bodhisattvas have little or no cultic presence apart from institutionally Buddhist forms of worship and thought. Conversely, Buddhism would have little or no independent institutional stature as a religion apart from its involvement with such buddhas and bodhisattvas. By contrast, yakshinis, even those whom Buddhists regard as spiritually advanced, may also have complex cultic lives apart from their place in the Buddhist pantheon.

The best-known narrative about the "naturalization" of a yakshini is that of an encounter between Hariti and Shakyamuni Buddha. (Though not a central figure in the *Splendid Vision*, Hariti is mentioned in sections 6 and 116.) As the story goes, Hariti was a human woman who, in a spiteful moment, vowed that she would become a yakshini in her next life and devour all the children in Rajgir, a town in northern India. True to her word she was reborn as a yakshini, gave birth to five hundred little yakshas of her own, and began to feast daily on Rajgir's babies. The mothers of the city cried out to Shakyamuni to save their children. To stop Hariti's rampage, Shakyamuni played a trick on her, stealing then hiding her favorite child. Hariti searched frantically for the boy. When at last she learned his whereabouts, Hariti demanded Shakyamuni return him to her eager arms. The buddha asked Hariti to reflect on the bitterness she felt, losing one of five hundred, and to compare her heartache with that of human mothers, who give birth to so few. Chastened, Hariti agreed to change her anthropophagic ways. In return for her sacrifice, the buddha promised that monks would feed Hariti and her children every day inside their monasteries. Indeed, shrines to Hariti became a standard feature of Buddhist monastic architecture. During their meal, monks would make offerings to Hariti, expecting, in return, that she would serve as a benefactress for the monks, the monastery, and the local community at large.

In this story, we see a monster, Hariti, who haunts a specific city, Rajgir, transformed into a beneficent deity whose superhuman power protects Buddhist monasteries and their lay supporters everywhere. As a yakshini, Hariti inhabits that intermediate ground between demoness and goddess, anger and compassion, harm and help, locality and universality.

Hariti was Indian Buddhism's most prominent yakshini. Anopama, Shankhini, and Bhima had far less renown. Nevertheless, we can guess that, structurally, they fit a generic pattern typified in Hariti's story: A divinity with a particular local identity is naturalized as a Buddhist divinity through a narrative of her taming and domestication. The closest evidence we have to support this hypothesis of the *Splendid Vision*'s yakshinis is an observation made by the Chinese traveler Xuanzang, who describes a shrine to a goddess named Bhima, located near modern-day Shahbazgarhi in Pakistan, approximately 180 miles southwest of Gilgit. At this shrine, Bhima was regarded as a great goddess and the wife of Shiva. Xuanzang describes her worship as follows:

> At more than fifty li to the northeast from Varsha, one reaches a lofty mountain, on which there is a bluish stone image of Bhima-devi, wife of Maheshvara [Shiva]. The local people said that this image of the goddess existed by nature. It showed many marvels and many people came to give prayers. In all parts of India, the people, noble and mean, who wish to pray

for blessedness flock to this place from far and near. Those who wish to see the physical form of the goddess may get a vision of her after fasting for seven days with a sincere and concentrated mind, and their wishes will in most cases be fulfilled.[59]

Is this Bhima identical to the *Splendid Vision*'s Bhima? Are they the "same" goddess seen by two pairs of eyes, one Hindu and one Buddhist? Did Buddhists have their own tale regarding Bhima's conversion, akin to that of Hariti? Certainly, the close correspondences in form, duration, and intent between Bhima's ritual as described by Xuanzang and her ritual as found in the *Splendid Vision* suggest a continuity between Buddhism and Hinduism in India's northwest of the sixth and seventh centuries.

To press these speculations one step further: the presence of a shrine to a great goddess named Bhima located along the ancient trans-Himalayan highway, not far from Gilgit, may help to clarify the history of the *Splendid Vision* itself. The introduction presented a capsule history of the sutra. There are three extant versions of the *Splendid Vision*: (1) the Gilgit manuscripts, dating to the sixth century; (2) a version from the Ganges River basin, translated by Yijing into Chinese in the seventh or eighth century; (3) a translation into Tibetan in the ninth century. We can leave (3) aside. For the particularly noteworthy fact here is that although (2) is one century younger than (1), (2) is also significantly shorter than (1). In fact, (2) includes only Shakyamuni's initial discourse and ritual; the remainder of the sutra is missing. Thus the *Splendid Vision* is preserved in two distinct manuscript traditions of significantly different lengths, associated with two significantly distant locations (about one thousand miles apart). The *Splendid Vision*'s original text is likely closer to (2) than to (1). The buddha's discourse probably constitutes the *Splendid Vision*'s original core, all the other incantations, rituals, and discourses added at a later date. Again, we cannot say when or where these additions were made. But—here is the salient point—the Buddhist pattern of converting local deities and appropriating their cults would suggest that the sections including

Anopama, Shankhini, and Bhima were added in locale(s) where these three yakshinis were significant divinities. The *Splendid Vision* would thus have served to naturalize and domesticate these yakshinis into the role of local bodhisattvas.

DEMONESS, BODHISATTVA

Let us now turn from these generalities to consider the *Splendid Vision*'s direct engagement with the three yakshinis. Anopama, Shankhini, and Bhima first appear in the sutra's opening tableau, introduced alongside other divine beings and superhuman entities (§§5–7). It is worth noting that although the entire heavenly realm seems to have emptied itself onto Potalaka Mountain, the yakshinis are the only divinities to be identified explicitly as bodhisattvas. The yakshinis may not have been the most powerful gods or goddesses in the pantheon, but for the *Splendid Vision* they were the most compassionate, which is to say, the most ready to place their superhuman power at the service of meeting deep human needs.

Incantations provide a prominent index of the yakshinis' compassionate activity. In effect, these incantations are the essence of the yakshinis' love, put into words, authorized as righteous by Shakyamuni, and given as gifts to all devotees who have faith in the buddha and do not doubt. By attending closely to the incantations' supplications and pleas we can illuminate the special nature of these yakshinis as bodhisattvas. (Note, the incantations are edited here to include only precative statements, i.e., statements that supplicate or entreat.)

> Anopama's incantation: Make all my endeavors succeed! Make my endeavors succeed! Give me success! Manifest your presence! Work your magic for me! Give me success! Fulfill all my hopes! (§70)

> Shankhini's incantation: Come! Stay! Make- make- maker of wealth! Make- make- maker of strength! Many different kinds of dresses and clothing! Pre- preserver of life! Pro- pro- protector of life! Remember the

tathagata! Remember your aspiration for awakening! Don't delay! Give me a gift! (§80)

Bhima's incantation: Obey the tathagata's command! Remember your promise. Give me a gift! Make me successful! (§87)

The most obvious point here is that yakshinis are associated with material well-being. Although Shankhini is the only yakshini to specify the worldly goods she will likely provide, all yakshinis are sought for mundane rather than transcendental benefits. Somewhat less predictably, each yakshini is asked to exercise her memory: *Remember the tathagata. Remember your oath. Remember your aspiration.* Why do we ask someone to remember? Because we are worried by the consequences in case she forgets. Indeed, these reminders make sense in light of yakshinis' figural ambivalence. Yes, Anopama, Shankhini, and Bhima are great bodhisattvas now. But once upon a time they had the potential to be ferocious baby-eating monsters. The incantations express anxiety that the yakshinis' oaths demarcate a thin red line separating their bodhisattvahood from their horrific other selves. In this light, it is also interesting that the yakshinis are not sought for protection from fiends and monsters, whereas such an appeal is made to the buddha and bodhisattvas. Perhaps this is because the yakshinis are viewed as half-dangerous creatures themselves, revered but never fully trusted.

To bring the particularity of the yakshinis' incantations into higher relief, we might compare them with those attributed to Shakyamuni, Avalokiteshvara, and Vajrapani. Again, the focus is on pleas and supplications. First, the buddha:

May the entire world be joyful! May previous karma be removed! May I be protected from every horror! (§30)

Of all the *Splendid Vision*'s incantations, Shakyamuni's is the shortest and most direct. Its statements emphasize the speaker's own sympathetic joy as well as her anxiety to be free of karma and its frightful effects—including, perhaps, encountering an untamed yakshini in a dark gully. There is no specific request here for liberation, though a compassionate attitude and freedom from karma both characterize the state of buddhahood.

The pleas of Anopama, Shankhini, and Bhima have little in common with that of the buddha. In the buddha's incantation, the human speaker adopts for herself the abstract compassionate attitude, "May the entire world be joyful." Addressing the buddha directly, the ritual performer takes on the persona of a bodhisattva. In the yakshinis' incantations, by contrast, the human practitioner relinquishes the role of bodhisattva and plays the part of supplicant. She has no need to represent her own compassion, because Anopama, Shankhini, and Bhima satisfy that role on her behalf. The ritual participant reminds the yakshinis that they have taken compassionate vows, expressed cosmic aspirations, and accepted burdensome obligations. She cautions: now that I need help, Anopama, Shankhini, Bhima, you had better not forget what you promised! In general, these incantations bespeak a close emotional reliance of the human practitioner upon the yakshinis. Entreaties like "do not delay," "manifest your existence," and "remember me" demonstrate a personal engagement lacking in the practitioner-buddha relationship as evidenced by his incantation.

Finally, if we look at Avalokiteshvara's and Vajrapani's incantations, we find them to be somewhat intermediate between those of the buddha and yakshinis.

Vajrapani's incantation: Obey the tathagata's command! Remember your promise! Destroy every sickness and every evil! Give me the gift of my choice! Whatsoever I request, may that be given to me in full! Save! Save! Come! Come! Please do not delay! Show your vajra body! (§38)

Avalokiteshvara's incantation: Look down, compassionate one! Focus on your aspiration for awakening! Look everywhere! Remember me! Remember the vow you made in the past! Through that vow, fulfill all my wishes! Purify a buddhafield! May no harm come to me! Remove my misdeeds of body, my misdeeds of speech, my misdeeds of mind! Remove my poverty!

Look out! Look across! Show! Show yourself to me! May all my merit grow!
Remember your promise, great one! (§56)

Like the buddha, the bodhisattva Avalokiteshvara is regarded as a
source of spiritual and worldly boons, a remover of bad karma. But
generally, the bodhisattvas have more in common with the yakshinis.
In each case, human practitioners directly appeal to emotions, while
the relationship with the buddha is more formal and distant. The bodhisattvas are implored to recollect their vows and reveal their presence. Like Avalokiteshvara, Shankhini is supposed to remember her
bodhisattva vow. Like Vajrapani, Bhima is supposed to heed her promise to the buddha to protect supplicants who recite her incantation.
Like both bodhisattvas, Anopama is supposed to give devotees success.

This difference between buddha and bodhisattvas/yakshinis as
cult figures is nicely captured in a verse from *The Questions of Kash-
yapa*, an early Mahayana sutra: "Just as people honor a new moon but
not the full moon, so my faithful [followers] should honor bodhisattvas with great intensity, but not me. Why? Because tathagatas are
born of bodhisattvas."[60] Let us add, on this logic, yakshinis deserve
deep veneration as well, for bodhisattvas are born of evildoers.

There is one additional trope by which the *Splendid Vision* marks
the bodhisattvahood of its yakshinis: a peculiar vow made by both
Anopama and Bhima at the end of their discourses. Consider Anopama's words. After presenting her incantation and ritual, Anopama
pledges,

> Blessed lord, if somebody performs this rite three times—even somebody
> guilty of the five atrocities that have immediate consequences—and if I do
> not respond, then may I not awaken to unsurpassed, complete, and perfect
> awakening. (§76; Bhima's parallel statement is at §92)

Frankly, I was startled when I first read this statement in the *Splendid Vision*. For at that time, I had seen a similar vow in only one other
sutra, *The Longer Sutra on the Land of Bliss*. That sutra tells the story
of a bodhisattva named Dharmakara who sets out to create the most

perfect buddhafield, one that is more ideal and excellent than all other buddhafields combined. Indeed, Dharmakara does succeed at creating this world, which he names Sukhavati, the Land of Bliss. Sovereign over the Land of Bliss is Amitabha, a buddha of infinite light born of Dharmakara's vows. Amitabha Buddha is immensely popular in China and Japan, in part because of a set of forty-seven vows recorded in *The Longer Sutra on the Land of Bliss*. In the sutra, Dharmakara utters these vows in order to describe his future buddhafield's perfection. This sutra and its vows are important here because Anopama's and Bhima's pledges in the *Splendid Vision* echo Dharmakara's vows, the shortest of which reads, "Blessed One, may I not awaken to unsurpassable, perfect, full awakening if living beings born in my buddha-field should not all be of one color, the color of gold."[61]

Although Dharmakara's words in the *Land of Bliss* sutra and Anopama's in the *Splendid Vision* are not precisely equivalent, there can be little doubt that the *Splendid Vision* is imitating the other sutra. The *Splendid Vision*'s author knew about the Land of Bliss: three times, it promises that someone who performs proper worship will be reborn in that Buddhist paradise (§§24, 34, and verses), and it mentions Amitabha Buddha once by name (verses). As cultured sixth-century Buddhists, Shulkshina and Shulivujna may well have heard echoes of Dharmakara's words in those spoken by Anopama. Recollecting this section's earlier discussion of performance and transformation, we can wonder whether Shulkshina and Shulivujna would have interpreted equivalences between Anopama's words and Dharmakara's words as an equivalence of the figures' characters. If Anopama vows in the same way as Dharmakara, does that mean she is also a bodhisattva after his model? In terms of performance theory, the answer is yes.

In an analysis of Dharmakara's vows, Luis Gómez has identified an important paradox, an odd logic that lends affective strength to the bodhisattva's vows. This paradox arises out of the fact that, although Dharmakara utters the words "may I not awaken to unsurpassable, perfect, full awakening" when he is still a bodhisattva, everybody in *The Longer Sutra on the Land of Bliss*'s audience knows that Dharmakara was fully enlightened long in the past, and that for aeons through to this very day he could be found in the Land of Bliss as Amitabha Buddha. In Gómez's words, "There could be no question in their minds that the vows had been fulfilled."[62]

We can apply this analysis to the *Splendid Vision* as follows: The resonances between Anopama's and Dharmakara's vows suggest that just as members of the sutra's audience were certain Dharmakara had perfected his vows, so they could be certain Anopama would always respond without fail. She definitely saves everybody who performs her rite three times. In this way, Anopama's rite—empowered by the buddhas, authorized by the buddhas—makes her a bodhisattva and certifies her own progress toward buddhahood. The affective charge inherent in Dharmakara's, Anopama's, and Bhima's paradoxical formulae is a variant on a common experience: when one tasty bite is left on a serving plate, everybody knows that the person who attempts to give it away the most forcefully is really the person who craves it the most. By offering to deny themselves buddhahood, Anopama and Bhima, like Dharmakara, performatively demonstrate the depth of their commitment to buddhahood. And by extension, they confirm the value and accuracy of the *Splendid Vision* (scriptural elements 1 and 2) as a basis for performance (no. 3).

AWAKENING IS TOO PRECIOUS TO WASTE ON THE AWAKENED

We have considered several ways in which Anopama, Shankhini, and Bhima act as bodhisattvas. But before we shift to this essay's conclusion, let me ask whether they ever act as yakshinis? After all, I have claimed that these three had their incantations and rituals appended to the *Splendid Vision* in order to appropriate their cults, and naturalize them within the Buddhist pantheon. Do we see any specific evidence, in these yakshinis' behaviors as described, of their having independent cults? The answer is no, if we look only at what Anopama, Shankhini, and Bhima themselves say and do. However, a brief glance at these yakshinis' roles in the *Splendid Vision*'s rituals tells a different story. All the rituals, except that described by Shakyamuni, require performers to cast bali offerings to the four directions. In general, the recipients of these bali offerings go unnamed, but in one case they are identified. Avalokiteshvara has performers of his rite "throw a bali offering of flavorful milk-rice and curd-rice to the four directions: to the goddess Bhima in the west, Anopama in the east, and Shankhini in the north" (§61). As the recipients of bali offerings, Bhima, Anopama, and Shankhini behave as common Indian yakshinis.

Bali offerings are not a uniquely Buddhist form of worship. In fact, the word *bali* designates a widespread ritual practice that seems to have been enjoined upon, and practiced by, all householders in ancient India, regardless of sectarian affiliation. These were offerings of rice, grain, barley, milk, or yogurt, given to feed the spirits of the dead and other potentially dangerous divinities who haunted the world by day and night. In the earlier story of Hariti, the buddha promises the yakshini that his monks will feed her in their monasteries. In pan-Indian terms, this is a statement that the monks will make a bali offering to Hariti every day. In Sanskrit, the word *bali* is also used to designate taxes paid to a king. This second meaning better helps to explain why bali offerings are so crucial and so prevalent. If a king's subjects do not pay their taxes, will he then just become a farmer and work the land himself? Rather, he will take that which he considers to be justly his by force of violence. Likewise, people must offer bali to their local yakshinis—providing the sweet, spicy, and alcoholic tastes they crave—for if the yakshinis are not sated, they will take what they want, preying upon oneself, one's family, and one's community. Although the *Splendid Vision* makes clear that Bhima, Anopama, and Shankhini could never revert to this feral state, the memory of their species nature as yakshinis is invoked by the association with the bali offering.

Recall Jerzy Grotowski, the Polish performance theorist introduced earlier. For Grotowski, a "holy actor" places her whole bodily existence at the service of her dramatic role, enacting her deep love for the world by presenting her physical self as a gift. With courage and skill, the holy actor reaches into the core of her emotional and psychic life, embodying her inner truths in the revelations of her face, the movements of her limbs, and the timbre of her voice. Anopama, Shankhini, and Bhima are holy actors: wild spirits who perform peace; voracious appetites who perform kindness; snatchers and ravagers who perform openhanded generosity. But they do ask their price. To receive the power of invisibility, wealth, fame, or any of the other worldly benefits the yakshinis would confer, a supplicant must also be willing to act: first by performing formal rites on the eighth day of the fortnight when the moon is waxing, but ultimately by embodying the ideals of the bodhisattva, just like the yakshinis themselves.

At heart, the *Splendid Vision* expresses Mahayana Buddhism's basic premise: *awakening is too precious to waste on the awakened.* As we have seen, the *Splendid Vision* strives to inspire audience members to accept the buddha's authority and, by extension, the sutra's own, since the *Splendid Vision* identifies itself as the buddha's current-day equivalent. In a more thorough reading, however, that is just a first step. To those who take it, the *Splendid Vision* then offers remarkable, life-changing practices: rites and incantations capable of giving one whatever one requests and making every wish come true. For those who accept the *Splendid Vision* as authoritative scripture, its status as a canonical expression of dharma, manifesting enlightened truths (elements 1 and 2), renders it a reliable guide to a happy and successful life (element 3).

Conclusion: On Impertinence

Last week, a friend asked me to translate the phrase "Choose the moment!" into Sanskrit and to write it down in Devanagari script. A day later, this mantra was tattooed on his left forearm. The timeliness of his request as I was finishing the book in turn set me thinking about other friends whose arms and wrists and necks and backs are indelibly marked with phrases scripted in languages they do not read, or with glyphs and abstract images whose symbolic meanings are private yet real. These are my friends. I cannot take so light an attitude toward them as I have toward the student who introduced this essay. They are a frivolous lot, but thoughtfully so: accomplished and intelligent, possessing advanced degrees and respected positions. I can certainly understand why someone would want an ever-visible mnemonic of his or her deep commitments. Symbolic couture is everywhere. From the crucifix or the Star of David on a necklace through the linked *C*s on Chanel sunglasses, we use abstractions to remind ourselves of who we are and want to be, while simultaneously displaying that ideal to others. But these tattoos differ from the commercial logos of multinational corporations or the icons of religions, in that they form an ostentatiously private language. At the moment, my friend is not committed to learning Sanskrit or its orthography. When he sees the swoops and swirls of Devanagari on his arm, he does not silently mouth the fluid sounds they represent but the heartfelt English imperative, Choose the moment! Why not write *that* on his arm? Why make so open a revelation in so covert a manner?

While puzzling over an answer, and at the same time contemplating the essay's conclusion, I was brought back to Marcel Duchamp's theory of the readymade. Recall from the introduction, Duchamp is remembered for having created art by recontextualizing everyday stuff. He attached a bicycle wheel to a kitchen stool to watch it spin; he bought a snow shovel at a hardware store and inscribed it, "In advance of the broken arm"; he signed and dated a porcelain urinal before installing it in a gallery.[63] For Duchamp, readymade art was an art of the mind not the eye. The beauty of the chosen object and its level of sophistication were beside the point. But while Duchamp did not choose objects for their aesthetic pleasure, he did modify them. Duchamp added verbal elements, like Richard Mutt's signature on *Fountain* and the humorous inscription on the snow shovel, in order to, in his words, "carry the mind of the spectator toward other regions more verbal."[64] Occasionally, when discussing readymades, Marcel Duchamp would wryly mock himself as an egomaniac. But Duchamp was not preaching his own gospel with these objects. If a commercially manufactured bicycle wheel, shovel, or urinal could become a work of art, it was only because somehow, by encountering them, a spectator entered a dissociative moment of unlearning, and became capable of beholding the everyday anew, as if for the first time. Duchamp chose objects and staged them for viewing. But a readymade only became art when it inspired a spectator to reinhabit his own life, notwithstanding Duchamp's ego.

Does this meditation on Duchamp clarify why my students and friends ink languages they do not speak onto their bodies using scripts they cannot read? Not really. It does remind me, however, that questions that begin with the word *why* are not always the right ones to ask. Inquiries that probe origins, reasons, and causes have their time. But sometimes one first needs to let go of all the uncertainties. And there is no way to accomplish *that* other than by first forgetting one's certainties: everything one knows, or might know, or wants to know, and most especially everything one knows that one does not know. Other curiosities peek through; other beauties await.

As a scholar, I have made a career of investigating linguistic nuance. Single letters, let alone whole words and phrases, are serious business for me. Minutiae matter. So at some level, it really does bother me when people tattoo themselves using languages and scripts in which they are unschooled. But simultaneously, I recognize that this is professional narcissism, which, left unchecked, must have a social cost. If, for me, the only legitimate use of Devanagari is communicating information in Sanskrit or Hindi—and if I extend this principle to all linguistic symbols—then I have no eyes to see the artistry of my friends' tattoos; no ears to hear about how their body art embodies values, truths, and meanings; no words with which to acknowledge that subcutaneous ink might serve them as a legitimate expression of authority or source of power. Blind, deaf, and dumb, I fail my friends. I fail to use the force of my intellect to confront the insularity of my own pieties, values, systems of truth, and behaviors. I fail to unlearn certainties. I fail to heed one of my own book's key insights: in line with the three elements of scripturality, any object can be scriptural as long as a community uses it as such. Failing to appreciate the profound gift my friends make to me with the splendid vision of their tattooed flesh, I fail to choose the moment, though it is ripe.

Thus I invoke Duchamp. By reframing symbolic tattoos as found art, I do not thereby gain a clear vision of the deeply particular significance each unique symbol embodies for its wearer. Quite the contrary, the act of reframing these symbols celebrates their material opacity, their conceptual density, and the fact that they do not give up their secrets, at first or second or even third glance. Are they pretty? Tasteful? Silly? Spelled correctly? Such judgments are beside the point. What matters is that I allow my eyes to open my spirit with impertinence, and then impertinently to appropriate these everyday objects as the material of conceptual art.

Though we commonly use the word *impertinence* as a synonym for rudeness and incivility, my use brings the word back to its Latin root: to pertain is "to hold through," to apply from end to end. Impertinence, here, is literally a state of not pertaining, not belonging, being unrelated or anomalous to a specific context. Readymade art is an art of interpretive impertinence. Look askew. Ask the wrong questions. But take the answers you receive as correct . . . at least for the moment. When I use my pertinent knowledge as a Sanskritist to analyze my friend's Devanagari tattoo, it seems a bit of folly. But allow me to enjoy the same thing with the impertinences of a friend and it rises to the level of art. Reframed as a readymade, his tattoo is thought provoking in ways that surprise and delight me as an interpreter. The word *devanagari* translates as "abode of the gods." Wearing a skin of Devanagari art, my friend literally embodies the language of gods in the world of men. I pair my knowledge with my imagination, and behold: he brings heaven to earth. A soft stream of divinized truisms burbles forth: Choose the moment! If not now, when? Be here now. My friend's tattoo truly is a splendid vision, for when I see it I never know what revelations will alight.

If a mere tattoo can accomplish this, then how much more so a formal scripture hallowed by tradition?

It is a common thing to tear down idols—especially other people's idols. It is a common thing to mock scriptures for their solemnities— especially other people's scriptures. It is a common thing to argue that, no matter whether the scripture is an ancient book or yesterday's tattoo, the investing of material objects with occult significance is an everyday occurrence—so much spiritual ostentation, nothing special. It is a common thing to feel your empathy is at its end. We are all outsiders.

Common though these things are, it is also possible to reframe them as prelude to something extraordinary. Each presents an opportunity for you to take responsibility for your own solemnities and ostentations, be they spiritual, intellectual, or physical. Each is an invitation to deep generosity; to make a total gift of yourself. For you to make that gesture, the act of reading must become an art of playful performance. Other people's opacity and impenetrability can be sources of great frustration. But with just a little expansiveness of spirit and imaginative impertinence, they are also occasions for connection, wonder, and joy.

In his writings and talks, Marcel Duchamp sometimes asked his audience to imagine a readymade that could never really be made: to use a Rembrandt as an ironing board.[65] Even a sublime object is still just an object and a work of genius can still be put to work. This is a book about that impossible act made possible.

GLOSSARY

AMITABHA (AMITĀBHA)   Literally, unlimited light. The buddha who created and dwells in the **Land of Bliss**. This name refers to the belief that
Amitabha is encircled by a halo of light, which spreads through and penetrates all universes without limit. It is also believed that Amitabha will
live forever. Thus other sutras also call him Amitayus, the buddha of im-
measurable life.

ANOPAMA (ANOPAMĀ)   Literally, without equal. A **yakshini** in the *Splendid Vision*.

ARHAT   Literally, worthy. A general term for any individual who frees himself from moral, psychic, and intellectual defects, especially desire, hatred,
and ignorance.

ASPIRATION TO AWAKEN AS A BUDDHA (CITTOTPĀDA)   Literally,
arising of the thought. Compassion—the wish that others should not suffer—is the emotional foundation of the **bodhisattva** path. As a technical
term, the *aspiration to awaken as a buddha* is the moment when this compassionate emotion is acted upon, and an individual consciously vows to
become a buddha in order to relieve the suffering of others.

ASURA   Literally, antigod. A kind of divinity who is overly proud and delights
in war. Although asuras have powers and life spans that far exceed those of
human beings, rebirth in this state is considered a **miserable rebirth** because asuras are so deeply in thrall to their passions.

AVALOKITESHVARA (AVALOKITEŚVARA)   Literally, the lord who
looked down. The best-known and most popular of Mahayana bodhisattvas, Avalokiteshvara resides on **Potalaka Mountain**. Modern litera-

ture on Buddhism often describes Avalokiteshvara as the bodhisattva of compassion.

BALI   Literally, tribute. A ritual offering made to dangerous spirits like yakshinis and ghosts. The offering of bali is not uniquely Buddhist. Traditional Hindu social codes require all householders to make five offerings, one of which is bali for the spirits. The Sanskrit word *bali* also designates taxes paid to a king. This helps to explain why bali offerings are so important. If a king's subjects do not pay their taxes, he has the right to seize their property by force. In this way, a king, who ought to protect his people, might attack them. Likewise, one must make a bali offering to yakshinis, providing foods they crave, like **curd-rice** and **milk-rice**. For yakshinis whose appetites are sated will protect human beings. But yakshinis who are not fed bali will instead eat children and other frail members of a community.

BHIMA (BHĪMĀ)   Literally, fearsome. Among the three great yakshinis presented in the *Splendid Vision*, Bhima seems to have been the best known. The seventh-century Chinese pilgrim Xuanzang describes a shrine to a goddess named Bhima, located near modern-day Shahbazgarhi in Pakistan, approximately 180 miles southwest of Gilgit. At this shrine, Bhima was regarded as a great goddess and the wife of Shiva.

BLESSED LORD (BHAGAVAT)   Literally, possessing fortune. An epithet for the buddha that emphasizes his status as a figure worthy of reverence and devotion. In Sanskrit literature, this term is also used for gods and kings.

BODHISATTVA   Literally, enlightenment being. A buddha-in-training. Somebody who has vowed to attain **unsurpassed, complete, and perfect awakening** in order to liberate himself and other beings from suffering.

BODHISATTVA MAHASATTVA (BODHISATTVA MAHĀSATTVA)   Literally, enlightenment being, great being. This epithet encapsulates the two qualities that bodhisattvas perfect while proceeding toward buddhahood. As an "enlightenment being," a bodhisattva strives to perfect the cognitive achievement of awakening: the full understanding of reality as-it-is. As a "great being," a bodhisattva strives to perfect the moral achievement of **great compassion**, the intention to free all creatures from samsara's suffering.

BODHISATTVA'S PERFECTIONS (PĀRAMITĀ)   Literally, gone to the other shore. The six principal virtues that a bodhisattva must perfect in order to become a complete and perfect buddha: generosity, morality, patient acceptance, energy, concentration, and wisdom.

BRAHMA (BRAHMĀ)   When used in the singular, Brahma is the universe's divine creator. When used in the plural, Brahma refers to any god that resides in one of the Brahma heavens, which living beings can reach by means of **samadhi** or **spiritual merit**. The creator-god Brahma resides in the Great Brahma Heaven, while other Brahma gods inhabit either the Brahma Assembly Heaven or the Brahma Minister Heaven. The Brahmas in these heavens are beyond desire and never perform evil acts.

BUDDHAFIELD (BUDDHA-KṢETRA)   Mahayana cosmology conceives of space abstractly, as an expanse of infinite magnitude filled with an incalculable number of individual universes, spreading out in all directions. Buddhas inhabit some of these universes, while others have no resident buddha. A universe in which a buddha resides is called a buddhafield. The buddha may be conceived as the supreme sovereign of his universe. Like an emperor, he is responsible for the welfare and happiness of all sentient beings born therein. And like an emperor, the limits of his direct personal authority and power are coextensive with the territorial limits of his buddhafield.

CAITYA   Literally, mounding. A memorial at which one can offer reverence to a buddha, arhat, or other religious figure.

CURD-RICE (DADHYODANA)   Literally, yogurt and boiled rice. A friend from India gave me the following recipe for this dish, prized for its cooling properties. Truly I do not know if this is how they made curd-rice in Gilgit:

1. Cook 2 cups basmati rice until very soft, even pasty, adding water as needed. Cool briefly.

2. Mash the rice well, slowly adding 1 to 1 1/2 cups plain yogurt, depending upon the consistency you prefer.

3. Add 1 tablespoon each finely chopped green chilies and finely chopped peeled fresh ginger.

4. Add 1/8 teaspoon asafetida (if available) and salt (to taste).

5. Heat 1 tablespoon oil in a small skillet over medium heat. Then fry 1 teaspoon black mustard seeds until they pop. Add to rice.

6. Stir ½ cup chopped fresh cilantro into the rice mixture.

7. Serve immediately. Or refrigerate for about an hour and serve.

DAKINI (ḌĀKINĪ)   A type of female demon who hunts the living and eats raw flesh.

DHARMA PREACHER (DHARMA-BHĀṆAKA)   An individual who propounds the dharma. In India, dharma preachers engaged in various preaching practices. Sometimes they recited sutras that they had memorized. At other times they gave religious discourses based upon their own insights or imaginations. Indeed, many sutras attributed to Shakyamuni, including the *Splendid Vision*, doubtless originated with such preaching. Dharma preachers could be lay or monastic, male or female. The *Splendid Vision* repeatedly instructs its audience to treat dharma preachers as they would Shakyamuni himself.

DISCIPLE (ŚRĀVAKA)   Literally, listener. A student who heard the buddha teach and followed him by becoming a renunciant. In Mahayana sutras like the *Splendid Vision*, disciples are monks and nuns who do not aspire to awaken as buddhas and thus are not self-identified as bodhisattvas.

EIGHT UPAVASA VOWS (AṢṬĀṄGOPAVĀSA)   Literally, eight-limbed fast. Buddhist laymen and laywomen are expected to adopt five prohibitions in their day-to-day lives: not to kill, steal, lie, engage in improper sexual conduct, or use intoxicants. However, on the eighth and fifteenth days of each fortnight, the particularly pious, or laity performing rituals like those detailed in the *Splendid Vision*, accept three additional behavioral restraints: (6) not to wear perfumes, garlands, or jewelry as well as not to sing or dance; (7) not to sleep on a high or broad bed; and (8) not to eat after the noon hour.

EXALTED RITE (UDĀRATARA-PŪJĀ)   Literally, higher worship. A common Mahayana ritual, having seven parts: (1) salutation to the buddhas, (2) making offerings to the buddhas, (3) confession of faults, (4) taking delight in others' merits, (5) asking the buddhas to teach the dharma, (6) aspiring to become a buddha oneself, and (7) sharing the spiritual merit gained through this performance with all living beings.

FIVE ATROCITIES THAT HAVE IMMEDIATE CONSEQUENCES (PAÑCĀNANTARYA)   Literally, five immediates. Generally, the karmic results of one's actions may ripen anytime in the future—perhaps in the next birth, perhaps in five births. But five deeds are so heinous that their karmic result must be experienced immediately upon their perpetrator's death. These five are killing one's own mother or father, killing an arhat, causing a schism in the sangha, and intentionally harming a buddha. A person guilty of any one of these five atrocities will necessarily be reborn in the lowest hell, Avici, in his very next life. The name Avici translates as "no release," for in this hell the torture never stops.

FOUR GREAT KINGS   A group of divine rulers, each of whom protects practitioners of dharma in one of the cardinal directions. Virudhaka, king of the kumbhandas (a type of demon so named because their testicles are as large as pots), protects the southern quarter. Virupaksha, king of the **nagas**, protects the western quarter. Vaishravana, king of the **yakshas**, protects the northern quarter. Dhritarashtra, king of the **gandharvas**, protects the eastern quarter.

GANDHARVA   A species of minor divinities who serve as celestial musicians and attendants to the **gods**. Gandharvas are usually pictured as hybrid beings, part human, part horse or bird.

GARUDA (GARUḌA)   A species of minor divinity possessing the beak and talons of a raptor combined with the head and torso of a human being—like a divine eagle.

GOD (DEVA)   A catchall term for beings that are more powerful than humans. In terms of the **three realms**, devas inhabit the upper reaches of the Realm of Desire; all beings in the Realm of Form and Realm of Formlessness are likewise considered devas. This is an inexact category. For instance, the *Splendid Vision* calls Bhima a "great goddess," even though yakshinis are earthbound divinities and thus do not inhabit a heaven.

GREAT COMPASSION (MAHĀ-KARUṆĀ)   In Buddhism, generally, compassion is defined as the desire for living beings to be free of suffering. Great compassion is the active implementation of this attitude, the acceptance of personal responsibility for freeing others. A bodhisattva mahasattva is an individual who not only thinks compassionate thoughts but also acts on them, by striving to become a buddha with the express purpose of freeing all from suffering.

HAUNTING GHOUL (PIŚĀCA)   Haunting ghouls are spirits of people who did not receive a proper funeral and thus are unable to proceed normally through the afterlife on the way to being reborn. Instead, haunting ghouls are stuck on earth as disembodied ghosts. They attack the living in the attempt to possess and inhabit our bodies. If you are at a cremation ground, don't yawn without covering your mouth. Haunting ghouls are invisible. They'll enter your throat and slide right down to your belly.

HUNGRY GHOST (PRETA)   Literally, deceased. A low rebirth, reserved for living beings deeply tormented by covetousness and greed. Hungry ghosts are usually envisioned as having mouths as small as pins and bellies as large as caverns. Everything they eat and drink turns to fire in their bellies. Thus even in satisfaction hungry ghosts are in torment.

INCANTATION (DHĀRAṆĪ)   Literally, sustainer. A spell or formula comprised of a string of syllables that give the person who writes or speaks them extraordinary powers. The *Splendid Vision* uses the terms *incantation* and *mantra* interchangeably.

INDRA   A principal god of the Vedic pantheon. For Buddhism, Indra is important as the king over a heaven in the Realm of Desire (*see* three realms). In this capacity, he is considered the paradigmatic protector of dharma as well as of those who practice dharma.

INNER FLOW OF THE MINDS AND MENTAL FACTORS (CITTA-CAITASIKA-SAṂMIṂJITA-PRASĀRITA)   This phrase has two parts. *Minds and mental factors* refers to the cognitive dimension of worldly existence. In brief, *mind* is a state of awareness or thought. *Mental factors* arise concurrently with mind, giving it content and affecting the quality of that content. These factors include such qualities as shamelessness, fear, tranquility, and the like. The Sanskrit rendered as *inner flow* translates literally as *retraction and extension*. Just as arms and legs can be stretched out and then drawn back, so the mind in all its complexity operates by attending to objects, and then withdrawing attention from them. Just as you can observe your friend reach out, pick up a glass, and lift it to her mouth so, according to the *Splendid Vision*, a bodhisattva empowered by all buddhas is able to read others' minds, observing thoughts themselves as well as the karmic qualities of those thoughts.

IN THE LAST TIME, IN THE LAST PERIOD (PAŚCIMA-KĀLE PAŚCIMA-SAMAYE)   An era of spiritual decline during which the buddha's teachings are still known but the doctrines are poorly understood and the precepts are largely ignored. There are no exact dates for the last time. However, the *Splendid Vision* encourages its audience to consider itself as living in this unfortunate period. The concept of "the last time" functions to situate and underscore the *Splendid Vision*'s claims of its own exalted authority and power, suggesting that anybody who willingly heeds its words in the period of spiritual decline must be an advanced bodhisattva.

KINNARA (KIṂNARA)   Literally, is it a man? A species of celestial being whose hybrid form has a human body topped by the head of a horse.

LAND OF BLISS (SUKHĀVATĪ)   This is the name of Amitabha's buddhafield; the **universe of three-thousand many-thousand worlds** over which he holds dominion. According to the *Land of Bliss* sutra, when Amitabha was still a bodhisattva he took several vows. One vow promised that there would be no difference between gods and human beings in the Land of Bliss. Another promised that everybody born in the Land of Bliss could remain there until he attains the final **stage on the bodhisattva path**. Thus to be reborn in the Land of Bliss is to guarantee that one will enjoy the bliss-filled life of a god until one attains buddhahood.

MAHORAGA   A species of celestial being whose hybrid form has a human body topped by the head of a snake.

MANDALA (MAṆḌALA)   Literally, circle. In general usage, a graphic representation of the cosmos, or cosmogram. In the *Splendid Vision*, a mandala is a space that has been consecrated for the purpose of ritual performance.

MANJUSHRI (MAÑJUŚRĪ)   A mythological bodhisattva. Mahayana texts often associate Manjushri with the perfection of wisdom and insight into ultimate reality. The *Splendid Vision* is not concerned with wisdom per se, but Manjushri's brief appearance demonstrates his perspicacity (at the beginning of the narrative, he sees and interprets an omen), as well as his intellectual curiosity (in the middle of the narrative, he interrogates Shakyamuni about the sutra's eponymous **samadhi**). Manjushri is often described as "princely" because, despite his ageless wisdom, he takes on the appearance of a sixteen-year-old prince.

MANTRA (MANTRA-PĀDA)   Literally, syllables of mantra. A verbal formula that holds spiritual or occult power. To access this power, one must utter the mantra in the context of an appropriate ritual. The *Splendid Vision* uses *mantra* interchangeably with *dharani*.

MILK-RICE (PĀYASA)   A pudding made with rice cooked in milk, also called *kheer*. A friend shared her recipe:

1. Wash and drain 1/2 cup basmati rice. Soak the rinsed rice in 1/2 cup water for 30 minutes.

2. Melt 1 tablespoon butter in a saucepan over medium heat. Add 4 whole cardamom pods. Stir once, then add the rice and soaking water to the pan. Leave uncovered and, without raising the heat, bring to a boil.

3. When the rice is coated and the water has evaporated (about 5 minutes; the rice will not be fully cooked), add 4 cups milk. Once the milk is steaming but not boiling, turn the heat to low. Simmer uncovered for 60 to 90 minutes. Lightly mash the rice and stir frequently to prevent sticking.

4. While the rice is cooking, soak several saffron threads in warm milk or water.

5. Heat 2 tablespoons butter in a skillet. Briefly cook 1/4 cup dried currants or raisins plus 1/4 cup unsalted cashews or pistachios until they are warm and aromatic. Transfer to a bowl and set aside.

6. When the milk-rice mixture is very thick and creamy, add 1 cup sugar. Stir well. Then add the saffron, currants, and nuts. Stir again and serve.

MISERABLE REBIRTHS (APĀYA)   Literally, going away. Realms of rebirth in which happiness is impossible. These include **Yama's realm**, the hells, the hungry ghost realm, rebirth as an animal, and rebirth among the asuras.

MISTAKENLY PERCEIVE PERMANENCE IN THE IMPERMANENT (ANITYE NITYA-SAṂJÑA)   This is one element in a traditional list of four misconceptions. Typically, the others include to mistakenly perceive purity in the impure; to mistakenly perceive satisfaction in the unsatisfactory; to mistakenly perceive selfhood in that which lacks a self. In keeping with the *Splendid Vision*'s lack of interest in ontology, however, the sutra presents a different, nontraditional, fourth misconception: to mistakenly perceive value in that which lacks inherent value.

MONSTER (AMANUṢYA)   Literally, nonhuman. This term can cover all nonhuman beings, from gods to demons. In context, however, it really means monster: a living creature that seems uncannily frightening and dangerous.

NAGA (NĀGA)   A class of divinity that takes the form of a serpent or cobra. Nagas are believed to have the particular ability to control rain—to bring the monsoon or cause a drought. Thus in agrarian India, nagas are a prominent focus of daily worship.

NĀṂ-TSE HAṂMĀRAPATI ŚŪLKṢIṆASYA ĀYSĀDIKA MAHĀŚRAD-DHOPĀSIKA ŚULIVUJÑASYA   This is an interpolation in several of the *Splendid Vision*'s mantras, indicating two individuals as the intended beneficiaries of their power. The exact meaning of the full phrase is not clear, but it seems to describe two people: a man named Shulkshina, and Shulivujna, a woman who was also a faithful lay devotee of the buddha.

NEVER STOP PROGRESSING TOWARD BUDDHAHOOD (PHYIR MI LDOG PA / AVAIVARTIKA). *See* stage on the bodhisattva path

OBSTACLES TO SPIRITUAL PROGRESS (ĀVARAṆA)   Literally, obstacle. Buddhists have long lists of obstacles to spiritual progress, including mental attitudes such as lust, sloth, uncertainty, anxiety, and so on. More generally, these obstacles split into two categories: moral obstacles and cognitive obstacles. The *Splendid Vision* focuses upon the former, in particular obstacles that arise as a result of evil actions or bad karma.

POTALAKA MOUNTAIN   Located near India's southern tip, this is the site of the *Splendid Vision*'s preaching. Avalokiteshvara is believed to reside in a stone palace on Potalaka's summit. Potalaka may be identified with Potiyil Mountain, near the town of Ambasamudram in the modern Indian state of Tamil Nadu. The Japanese scholar Shu Hikosaka has hypothesized that the word *potalaka* is a corruption of the Sanskrit *bauddha-loka*, literally, "the place of the Buddhists." Because the Dalai Lama of Tibet is deemed an incarnation of Avalokiteshvara, his palace-temple in Lhasa is also called Potala.

PROPHECY THAT HE OR SHE WOULD BECOME A BUDDHA (VYĀKARAṆA)   Literally, explanation. A significant moment on the bodhisattva's path to buddhahood. The prophecy is received from a buddha when he declares that a particular bodhisattva will attain unsurpassed, complete, and perfect awakening in the future. The bodhisattva also learns his future name as a buddha, his caste, how long he will live, as well as other sundry information. Since buddhas cannot make mistakes, a bodhisattva who receives this prophecy is receiving an absolute guarantee of his own future buddhahood.

PUJA (PŪJĀ)   Literally, worship. A general term for rituals that express devotion, veneration, or homage.

RECEPTIVE TO THE TRUTH THAT PHENOMENA NEITHER COME INTO EXISTENCE NOR CEASE TO EXIST (ANUTPATTIKEṢU DHARMEṢU KṢĀNTI)   Literally, patient acceptance vis-à-vis the nonarising of phenomena. A central doctrine of Mahayana Buddhism. The second part of the term—the nonarising of phenomena—describes the fundamental nature of reality. According to traditional Buddhist doctrine, all worldly phenomena arise and exist in dependence upon causes. The Mahayana philosophy of emptiness takes this insight to its logical limit, positing that all causes and conditions are empty: nothing is self-originated; nothing is brought into existence by something other than itself; nothing is caused by both itself and something else; and nothing exists totally without a cause. So, if all worldly phenomena are necessarily produced through causes, but no absolute cause can be shown for any of them, then no worldly phenomenon can be said to have substantial existence. If phenomena do not have a substantial existence then, logically, they also cannot cease to exist. I gloss the first part of the term as "receptive." The literal translation for this Sanskrit word is "patience" or "tolerance." It is not easy to stomach a doctrine that denies the solid reality of the everyday world in which we live. For Buddhism, it is not sufficient to understand this truth with one's intellect. When fully grasped this truth has a profound emotional impact. One must accept this truth with conviction, becoming receptive to its startling implications.

RELIC (DHĀTU)   Literally, constituent. Interest in relics goes back to the time of Shakyamuni himself. After the buddha was cremated, the remaining pieces of charred bone were gathered and interred in several **stupas**, allowing the buddha to still participate in the community bodily, now as an object of worship. Eventually Buddhists came to allow that other things might serve as functional equivalents for the buddha's bodily relics. Other categories of relic include *contact relics* (objects that the buddha used or owned, such as his bowl, robes, bodhi tree) and *dharma relics* (texts that reproduce the dharma: from an entire sutra to an incantation). The *Splendid Vision* does not stipulate which kind of relic it intends, but dharma relics were the type most readily available.

ROOTS OF VIRTUE (KUŚALA-MŪLA)   General term for bodily acts, utterances, and mental states that create either spiritual merit or another form of spiritual advancement. Like the roots that nourish a plant or tree, these roots of virtue bring forth beautiful flowers and fruits: exalted rebirths, happiness, and progress along the bodhisattva path.

SAMADHI (SAMĀDHI)   Literally, putting together. A state of deep meditative absorption, within which the mind is fully concentrated on a single point of focus. As we see in the *Splendid Vision*, such concentrated states are neither static nor devoid of content. A mind in samadhi is so dynamic and powerful that its visionary experiences are able to transform the world outside the meditator's mind.

SHANKHINI (ŚAṄKHINĪ)   Literally, shell woman. There is not much to say about this yakshini beyond what one reads in the *Splendid Vision*. Female divinities named Shankhini are found in two other Buddhist Sanskrit works. The *Mahamayuri* includes this name in a list of flesh-eating demonesses; the *Kalacakra Tantra* names a Shankhini as a divine consort. However, we cannot say for certain whether either of these is the "same" Shankhini as the sutra's yakshini.

SITUATIONS UNFAVORABLE FOR PRACTICING DHARMA (AKṢAṆA)   Literally, untimely. There are eight unfavorable situations in which to be born. The first seven occur when, although a buddha is alive, you do not have access to him because you are in hell, or an animal, or a hungry ghost, or a god, or a human being born into a borderland or foreign region, or a human being who lacks vision, hearing, or some other necessary sense faculty, or finally you are just plain stupid. The eighth unfavorable birth is that of a human being who has enough receptivity and intelligence to learn dharma but who is born at a time when no buddha is present to instruct him.

SOLITARY BUDDHA (PRATYEKA-BUDDHA)   Literally, awakened alone. Like an arhat, a solitary buddha is free of desire, hatred, and ignorance and thus is liberated from samsara. But the solitary buddha has no teacher and, in turn, takes no disciples. He is a hermit, who realizes the truth for himself and enjoys freedom by himself.

SON OF GOOD FAMILY / DAUGHTER OF GOOD FAMILY (KULA-PU-TRA / KULA-DUHITṚ)   A member of the Buddhist community. Someone who vows Buddhist vows, practices Buddhist practices, values Buddhist ideals, and aspires after Buddhist goals. The term *son of good family* denotes a religious affiliation but also bespeaks social status. According to the classic Indian jurisprudence, a king is obligated to protect people in his domain. But India recognized that castes, tribes, and families also had their own particular, internal laws. The king's job, therefore, was to make sure that families could regulate themselves effectively. So by indicating that an individual belongs to the Buddhist family, *son of good family* also names him or her as subject to Buddhist laws. In short, a son of good family's public identity expresses his allegiance to the buddha. Finally, *son of good family* is also a term of affection: it expresses affirmation and love for a person as well as the life choices he or she has made.

SORCERER (VIDYĀ-DHARA) Literally, holder of knowledge. A practitioner of magic. A master at wielding the cosmic power contained in incantations and mantras.

SOURCES FROM WHICH KARMA STREAMS FORTH (ĀSRAVA) Literally, streaming forth. This is a gloss on a term that is often translated as "depravity" or "outflow." Commonly, the four sources of karma are listed as the objects of sense pleasure, the desire for existence, mistaken views, and ignorance.

SPIRITUAL MERIT (PUṆYA) The technical term for what is often referred to as good karma. Spiritual merit is the positivity that accrues to an individual as a result of positive actions, whether they are deeds of generosity, worship, morality, or mental concentration. Spiritual merit is often treated as a kind of spiritual capital that, like money, can be exchanged, given away, and invested. On this model, the *Splendid Vision* presents itself as a source of unparalleled dividends for those who invest in it. Unlike money, however, you can take spiritual merit with you after you die.

STAGE ON THE BODHISATTVA PATH (BODHISATTVA-BHŪMI) The Mahayana has various schemas for describing the stages through which a bodhisattva progresses from the first moment at which he aspires to awaken as a buddha through the final moment, in which he attains the unsurpassed, complete, and perfect awakening of a buddha. One such schema presents this path as having ten stages. The *Splendid Vision* takes a particular interest in the eighth and tenth of these stages. The eighth stage—called the Immovable—is crucial because a bodhisattva who reaches this stage can never backslide from progressing toward buddhahood. He is destined to become a buddha and everything he does from thereon will foster his progress. The tenth stage—called the Cloud of Dharma—is significant because it represents the bodhisattva's final plateau before buddhahood.

STUPA (STŪPA) A memorial containing the relics of a buddha or other religious figure. Early India stupas were hemispherical in shape, with relics interred in the heart of the monument. Later, the stupa form became more varied, including cones and stepped pyramids.

SUGATA Literally, well gone. An epithet of the buddha emphasizing felicity.

SUPREME FINAL NIRVANA (MAHĀ-PARI-NIRVĀṆA) Literally, all-encompassing extinguishment. The complete transcendence of karmic bondage and thus of suffering.

TATHAGATA (TATHĀGATA) Literally, thus come/thus gone. A title that Shakyamuni commonly uses when referring to himself or other buddhas. The Sanskrit word *tathagata* can translate either as "thus come" or "thus gone." Because of this indeterminacy, the term tends to mystify the buddha's identity and thereby preclude all further investigation into Shakyamuni's nature as buddha. If one asks, how does a buddha come into the world? the answer is: thus! In just the way Shakyamuni does! If one asks, how does a buddha leave the world? the answer is: thus! In just the way that Shakyamuni does! In short, whereas the epithet "blessed lord" accentuates venerability, the epithet "complete and perfect buddha" accentuates insight, and the epithet "sugata" accentuates felicity, the epithet "tathagata" accentuates mystery and transcendence.

TEN DIRECTIONS (DAŚA-DIŚA) East, southeast, south, southwest, west, northwest, north, northeast, above, below.

THREE JEWELS (TRI-RATNA) Buddha, dharma, and sangha. Buddhism's existential ideal, Buddhism's doctrinal truths, Buddhism's social organization.

THREE REALMS (TRAI-DHĀTUKA) A world system in its entirety is composed of three realms: a Desire Realm, a Form Realm, and a Formless Realm. The Desire Realm includes hells, the domains of the hungry ghosts, animals, humans, as well as Desire Heavens, including the heaven of Indra and those of the four great kings. In the Desire Realm, living beings are motivated by the passions, lust, greed, anger, malice, and ignorance. Beyond the Desire Realm lies the Realm of Form, a state that can be attained through samadhi or the accumulation of spiritual merit. Although beings in the Form Realm enjoy bliss without desire, they are, nevertheless, encumbered by materiality. The Brahma gods live in the Form Realm. Beyond the Form Realm is the Realm of Formlessness, attained only by means of samadhi. Here, beings have neither desire nor materiality. The "pinnacle of existence" is found at the very apex of this Formless Realm.

UNIVERSE OF THREE-THOUSAND MANY-THOUSAND WORLDS (TRI-SĀHASRA-MAHĀ-SĀHASRA LOKA-DHĀTU) Buddhists had many schemas for structuring the cosmos. The three-thousand-fold many-thousand-fold universe is the largest single unit. In Mahayana literature it is the equivalent of a buddhafield. To calculate the size of such a universe, one begins with a single world system (composed of the three realms). One thousand world systems make a "small thousand." One thousand of these "small thousand" world systems (i.e., $1,000^2$) is called a medium thousand. One thousand of these "medium thousand" world systems (i.e., $1,000^3$) is called a great thousand. One billion worlds is modest in scope given the discoveries of contemporary astronomy. If you are of a literal bent, accordingly, imagine how much space would be needed, not to find one billion worlds but to find one billion worlds each of which is inhabited by intelligent and self-conscious life-forms. Why bother? Because the universe of three-thousand many-thousand worlds should be conceptualized in terms of its sense of sheer immensity, as well as its specific number.

UNSURPASSED, COMPLETE, AND PERFECT AWAKENING (ANUTTARA-SAMYAK-SAMBODHI) The fullest possible insight into the nature and substance of reality. There are several possible degrees of awakening. This is the awakening of a complete and perfect buddha; as such it surpasses the awakenings of the disciple and the solitary buddha.

VAJRA Literally, lightning/diamond. Ancient Indians believed that lightning was made of diamond—a hard, glowing, translucent mineral. Thus the vajra came to symbolize the active principle of dharma, which is spontaneous, supremely potent, and indestructible. The vajra is also conceived of as a weapon. In Vedic mythology, Indra wielded the vajra when battling the gods' enemies. For Buddhism, the vajra is a weapon wielded by Vajrapani to destroy demons and the buddha's foes.

VAJRADHARA Literally, vajra holder. In the *Splendid Vision*, this is another name for **Vajrapani**. In Tantric Buddhism, Vajradhara becomes an important buddha in his own right.

VAJRAKRODHA Literally, vajra wrath. A bodhisattva, perhaps another name for **Vajrapani**. Wrath here is not anger—a karmic poison—but the forceful attitude that bodhisattvas adopt in order to destroy the obstructions and ignorance that impede progress along the path to buddhahood.

VAJRAPANI (VAJRA-PĀṆI) Literally, vajra-in-hand. Unlike Avalokiteshvara and Manjushri, Vajrapani had a prominent role in Buddhist mythology before the advent of the Mahayana. For early Buddhism, Vajrapani was a yaksha who served as Shakyamuni's bodyguard. Holding a diamond-hard vajra as a weapon, Vajrapani threatened to crush the head of anybody who abused the buddha. With the Mahayana, Vajrapani became an important bodhisattva. Building upon his early symbolism, however, the bodhisattva Vajrapani continued to play the role of guardian. He protects less-powerful bodhisattvas and practitioners of dharma from all harm.

WILD DEMON (RĀKṢASA)   Literally, to be protected against. A species of demon that haunts the wilds at night and eats human flesh. Wild demons can take the form of almost any other creature, from a jackal, to an eagle, to one's own beloved. In their natural forms, however, wild demons have glowing red eyes and long lolling tongues.

WORLD SYSTEM (LOKA-DHĀTU). *See* buddhafield; three realms; universe of three-thousand many-thousand worlds.

YAKSHA (YAKṢA)   The male equivalent of a yakshini.

YAKSHINI (YAKṢIṆĪ)   A wide-ranging class of female divinities. Yakshinis are forces of fertility, wielding control over the waters, the fields, and the forests of the natural world, as well as over human and animal fecundity, life, and death. Yakshinis are often described as ambivalent deities because they can create abundance or lay famine across the land; they can bring robust health or plague. Thus, the boundaries of *yakshini* as a category of superhuman being are not precise. On the one hand, yakshinis overlap with haunting ghouls and wild demons. On the other hand, as we see in the *Splendid Vision*, yakshinis might also be celebrated as great goddesses and spiritually advanced bodhisattvas.

YAMA'S REALM (YAMA-LOKA)   Yama, the god of death, has a complex mythology that predates the advent of Buddhism in India. As represented by the *Splendid Vision*, Yama is the lord over the hells, a realm of unmitigated suffering and terror that exists beneath the earth.

NOTES

Preface

1   See Cohen 2010 for a technical introduction to the *Splendid Vision* and transcriptions of its Sanskrit manuscripts.
2   Cohen 2006.

Introduction to the Translation

1   Jettmar 1981, 6. The earliest reports of the Gilgit manuscripts are found in Stein 1931, Lévi 1932, and Shastri 1939.
2   Fussman 2004, 134.
3   Chandra 1959.
4   The phrase "splendid vision" translates the complete title's final element, *vyūha*.
5   Cohen 2010 offers a longer discussion of each manuscript, as well as a concordance of the Sanskrit, Tibetan, and Chinese versions.
6   von Hinüber 1981.
7   Bourdieu 1988, 21.
8   Duchamp 1989, 194.
9   A happy coincidence. Soon after *Fountain* was rejected by the exhibition in New York, *The Blind Man*, a leading dadaist magazine, published a defense of the work. The article's title: "Buddha of the Bathroom" (Norton 1917).
10 Vatsyayana 2008, verse 1.3.6.
11 The corresponding Tibetan is also included in Cohen 2010.

Translation

1   As noted in the introduction, the Sanskrit manuscripts of the *Splendid Vision* are missing their first leaves. Prior to this point, the translation is based on the Tibetan version; after this point, the Sanskrit.

Interpretive Essay

1   Aristotle 1941, 881 (*Metaphysics* 1073a).
2   Segal 1983.
3   Ibid., 109.
4   Ibid., 114.
5   Ibid.
6   The bibliography on this subject is quite large. The following suggestions are not meant to be exhaustive. For an overview of cognitive dissonance theory, see Cooper 2007. For a philosophical introduction to the implications of cognitive science, see Lakoff and Johnson 1999. Additional noteworthy studies include Wilson 2002 and Wegner 2002. For more recent works, see Clark 2008, Noë 2009, and Chemero 2009.
7   Two accessible works in this field are Lewis, Amini, and Lannon 2001 and Cozolino 2006.
8   Wilson 2002, 23.
9   Martin Luther, cited in Grant 1952, 131.
10 Luther 2003, 170.
11 Although for obvious reasons I focus on scriptures as written texts, in fact anything can function as scripture: books, stories, objects, people, songs, performances, maps, even concepts. See Wimbush 2008 for an expanded discussion of scripture beyond books.
12 Olin 1966, 39.
13 Ibid., 54.
14 Ibid., 55.
15 To be more precise, the medieval quadriga posited a fourfold sense of scripture: (1) the literal sense (i.e., taking statements at face value); (2) the allegorical sense (i.e., reading the Bible for confirmation of doctrinal truths), (3) the tropological sense (i.e., reading the Bible for moral teachings and practices), (4) the anagogical sense (i.e., reading the Bible for promises of future salvation).

16 Luther 2003, 192.

17 Martin Luther, cited in Ramm 2001, 54.

18 Luther 2003, 73–74.

19 Calvin 1960, 2:980.

20 On this phrase as a guarantor of authenticity, see Galloway 1991, Tola and Dragonetti 1999.

21 Strong 1995, 37.

22 Ibid.

23 Lamotte 1981, 101.

24 Galloway 1991, 89.

25 Barthes 1972, 142.

26 The best general introductions to Avalokiteshvara can be found in Holt 1991 and Studholme 2002.

27 These stories and more can be found in Studholme 2002.

28 Xuanzang 1996, 322.

29 Hikosaka 1989, 185.

30 Asaṅga 1978, 2.

31 Dutt 1931, 275.

32 Vasubandhu 1987, 187.

33 Gnoli 1977, 2:262.

34 Suzuki 1955–1962, 44:156, folio 4 (Peking bKa'-'gyur 'dul ba Ne 86a5 to 86a6).

35 Gethin 1997, 211.

36 Gómez 1996, 323.

37 Gnoli 1977, 1:137.

38 This discussion is based upon Lincoln 1994, 38–40.

39 "Excerpts from Interview with Nixon About Domestic Effects of Indochina War," *New York Times*, May 20, 1977, A16.

40 Calvin 1960, 2:949.

41 Lincoln 1994, 11.

42 Ibid., 12.

43 See Kant 1999, especially *Groundwork of The Metaphysics of Morals* and *Critique of Practical Reason*.

44 One particularly good and recent work in this genre is Baer, Kaufman, and Baumeister 2008.

45 Cozolino 2006, 240.

46 Lewis, Amini, and Lannon 2001, 76.

47 Burton 2008, 125.

48 Bloom 2010, 207.

49 Ibid., 9.

50 Ibid., 22.

51 Gnoli 1977, 1:118.

52 Fischer-Lichte 2008, 78.

53 Grotowski 2002, 35.

54 Ibid., 19.

55 Ibid., 16.

56 Note the close similarity between the *Splendid Vision*'s claim in this passage and Luther's claim (cited on p. 65) that unless one is touched by the holy spirit one cannot really comprehend the Bible.

57 Fischer-Lichte 2008, 84.

58 Shaw 2006, 62.

59 Xuanzang 1996, 79–80.

60 von Staël-Holstein 1926, 129.

61 Gómez 1996, 69.

62 Ibid., 37.

63 Duchamp 1989, 141.

64 Ibid.

65 Ibid., 32, 142.

WORKS CITED

Aristotle. 1941. *Metaphysics*. In *The Basic Works of Aristotle*, ed. Richard McKeon, 681–926. New York: Random House.

Asaṅga. 1978. *Bodhisattvabhūmi*. Ed. Nalinaksha Dutt. Patna: Kashi Prasad Jayaswal Research Institute.

Baer, John, James C. Kaufman, and Roy F. Baumeister, eds. 2008. *Are We Free? Psychology and Free Will*. New York: Oxford University Press.

Barthes, Roland. 1972. *Mythologies*. Trans. Annette Lavers. New York: Hill & Wang.

Bloom, Paul. 2010. *How Pleasure Works: The New Science of Why We Like What We Like*. New York: Norton.

Bourdieu, Pierre. 1998. *On Television*. Trans. Priscilla Parkhurst Ferguson. New York: Free Press.

Burton, Robert. 2008. *On Being Certain: Believing You Are Right Even When You're Not*. New York: St. Martin's Press.

Calvin, Jean. 1960. *Institutes of the Christian Religion*. Ed. John T. McNeill. Trans. Ford Lewis Battles. Philadelphia: Westminster Press. (Orig. pub. 1536.)

Chandra, Lokesh. 1959. "A Note on the Gilgit Manuscripts." *Journal of the Oriental Institute* (University of Baroda) 9:135–40.

Chemero, Anthony. 2009. *Radical Embodied Cognitive Science*. Cambridge, Mass.: MIT Press.

Clark, Andy. 2008. *Supersizing the Mind: Embodiment, Action, and Cognitive Extension*. New York: Oxford University Press.

Cohen, Richard S. 2006. *Beyond Enlightenment: Buddhism, Religion, Modernity*. Oxford: Routledge.

——. 2010. "The Sarvatathāgatādhiṣṭhāna-satvāvalokana-buddhakṣetra-sandarśana-vyūha: A Mahāyāna Sūtra from Gilgit." *Indian International Journal of Buddhist Studies* 11:199–251.

Cooper, Joel. 2007. *Cognitive Dissonance: Fifty Years of a Classic Theory*. London: Sage.

Cozolino, Louis. 2006. *The Neuroscience of Human Relationships: Attachment and the Developing Social Brain*. New York: Norton.

Duchamp, Marcel. 1989. *The Writings of Marcel Duchamp*. Ed. Michel Sanouillet and Elmer Peterson. New York: Da Capo Press.

Dutt, Nalinaksha. 1931. "Bodhisattva Prātimokṣa Sūtra." *Indian Historical Quarterly* 7:259–86.

Fischer-Lichte, Erika. 2008. *The Transformative Power of Performance: A New Aesthetics*. Trans. Saskya Iris Jain. London: Routledge.

Fussman, Gérard. 2004. "Dans quel type de bâtiment furent trouvés les manuscrits de Gilgit?" *Journal asiatique* 292:101–50.

Galloway, Brian. 1991. "'Thus Have I heard: At One Time . . .'" *Indo-Iranian Journal* 34, no. 2:87–104.

Gethin, Rupert. 1997. "Cosmology and Mediation: From the Agañña Sutta to the Mahāyāna." *History of Religions* 36:183–217.

Gnoli, Raniero, ed. 1977. *The Gilgit Manuscript of the Saṅghabhedavastu, Being the Seventeenth and Last Section of the Vinaya of the Mūlasarvāstivādin*. Rome: Istituto Italiano per il Medio ed Estremo Oriente.

Gómez, Luis O. 1996. *The Land of Bliss: The Paradise of the Buddha of Measureless Light*. Honolulu: University of Hawai`i Press.

Grant, Robert. 1952. *A Short History of the Interpretation of the Bible*. Philadelphia: Fortress Press.

Grotowski, Jerzy. 2002. *Towards a Poor Theatre*. Ed. Eugenio Barba. New York: Routledge.

Hikosaka, Shu. 1989. *Buddhism in Tamilnadu: A New Perspective*. Madras: Institute of Asian Studies.

Holt, John. 1991. *Buddha in the Crown: Avalokiteśvara in the Buddhist Traditions of Sri Lanka*. New York: Oxford University Press.

Jettmar, Karl. 1981. "The Gilgit Manuscripts: Discovery by Installments." *Journal of Central Asia* 4, no. 2:1–18.

Kant, Immanuel. 1999. *Practical Philosophy*. Ed. Mary Gregor. Cambridge: Cambridge University Press.

Lakoff, George, and Mark Johnson. 1999. *Philosophy in the Flesh: The Embodied Mind and Its Challenge to Western Thought*. New York: Basic Books.

Lamotte, Étienne. 1981. *Le traité de la grande vertu de sagesse de Nāgārjuna (Mahāprajñāpāramitāśāstra)*. Vol. 1. Leuven: Peeters.

Lévi, Sylvain. 1932. "Note sur des manuscrits sanscrits provenant de Bamiyan (Afghanistan) et de Gilgit (Cachemire)." *Journal asiatique* 220:1–45.

Lewis, Thomas, Fari Amini, and Richard Lannon. 2001. *A General Theory of Love*. New York: Vintage.

Lincoln, Bruce. 1994. *Authority: Construction and Corrosion*. Chicago: University of Chicago Press.

Luther, Martin. 2003. *The Bondage of the Will*. Trans. J. I. Packer and O. R. Johnston. Grand Rapids: Revell. (Orig. pub. 1525.)

Noë, Alva. 2009. *Out of Our Heads: Why You Are Not Your Brain, and Other Lessons from the Biology of Consciousness*. New York: Hill & Wang.

Norton, Louise. 1917. "The Richard Mutt Case: Buddha of the Bathroom." *Blind Man* 2:5–6.

Olin, John C., ed. 1966. *A Reformation Debate: Sadoleto's Letter to the Genevans and Calvin's Reply*. New York: Harper & Row.

Ramm, Bernard. 2001. *Protestant Biblical Interpretation*. Grand Rapids: Baker Books.

Segal, Robert A. 1983. "In Defense of Reductionism." *Journal of the American Academy of Religion* 51, no. 1:97–124.

Shastri, M. S. Kaul. 1939. "Report on the Gilgit Excavation in 1938." *Quarterly Journal of the Mythic Society* 30, no. 1:1–12, plus plates.

Shaw, Miranda. 2006. *Buddhist Goddesses of India*. Princeton: Princeton University Press.

Stein, Aurel. 1931. "Archaeological Discoveries in the Hindukush." *Journal of the Royal Asiatic Society of Great Britain and Ireland*, 863–65.

Strong, John. 1995. *The Experience of Buddhism: Sources and Interpretations*. Belmont, Calif.: Wadsworth.

Studholme, Alexander. 2002. *The Origins of Oṃ Manipadme Hūṃ: A Study of the Kāraṇḍavyūha Sūtra*. Albany: SUNY Press.

Suzuki, Daisetz Teitaro, ed. 1955–1962. *The Tibetan Tripitaka: Peking Edition*. Tokyo: Tibetan Tripitaka Research Institute.

Tola, Fernando, and Carmen Dragonetti. 1999. "Ekam Samayam." *Indo-Iranian Journal* 42, no. 1:53–55.

Vasubandhu. 1987. *Abhidharmakośa and Bhāṣya of Ācārya Vasubandhu with Sphūṭārthā Commentary of Ācārya Yaśomitra*. Ed. Dwarikadas Sastri. Varanasi: Bauddha Bharati.

Vatsyayana. 2008. *Kāma Sutra*. Ed. Mizue Sugita and Jost Gippert. http://titus.uni-frankfurt.de/texte/etcs/ind/aind/klskt/kamasutr/kamas.htm (accessed June 18, 2010).

von Hinüber, Oskar. 1981. "Namen in Schutzzaubern aus Gilgit." *Studien zur Indologie und Iranistik* 7:163–71.

von Staël-Holstein, Alexander, ed. 1926. *The Kāśyapaparivarta: A Mahāyānasūtra of the Ratnakūṭa Class*. Shanghai: Commercial Press.

Wegner, Daniel M. 2002. *The Illusion of Conscious Will*. Cambridge, Mass.: MIT Press.

Wilson, Timothy D. 2002. *Strangers to Ourselves: Discovering the Adaptive Unconscious*. Cambridge, Mass.: Harvard University Press.

Wimbush, Victor L., ed. 2008. *Theorizing Scriptures: New Critical Orientations to a Cultural Phenomenon*. Rutgers: Rutgers University Press.

Xuanzang. 1996. *Great Tang Dynasty Record of the Western Regions*. Trans. Li Rongxi. Berkeley: Numata Center.

INDEX